Death of the Docks

Colin Ross

AuthorHouse™ UK Ltd.
500 Avebury Boulevard
Central Milton Keynes, MK9 2BE
www.authorhouse.co.uk
Phone: 08001974150

© 2010 Colin Ross. All rights reserved.

No part of this book may be reproduced, stored in a retrieval system, or transmitted by any means without the written permission of the author.

First published by AuthorHouse 5/25/2010

ISBN: 978-1-4520-1909-3 (sc)

This book is printed on acid-free paper.

Introduction

Many books have been written about both the east end of London and the dock industry, mostly by people who know absolutely next to nothing about either the area or the people who made the east end of London the place it was, as for the dock industry nearly all of them knew next to nothing about an industry that time seemed to have forgot. In fact you could quite easily get what they actually know about the docks on the back of a postage stamp. I hope that this book will help to explain the highs and lows of life on the docks; also I hope it will explain how the system is stacked against you, and how the government finally shafted us. Many original East Enders have been forced to move out of the area that they and generations of their families before them were born in. The reason for this is the emergence of the property speculator, who 20 years ago would not have been seen dead in the area, and coupled with their arrival the massive change of people who proclaim to be the new east enders. Luckily for some of the real east Enders they bought their council home and watched the value of property soar, this gave them their chance to escape. Having seen the area that 3 or more generations of their family grew up and lived in had changed beyond recognition, it was time to get out.

Not only had we had our neighbourhood stolen from us but many people felt that they had lost their identity. But this only all happened after the closure of the areas main industry -the docks. So nearly all of them decided to sell up and move away. This not only broke up communities but also saw the breakdown of family life as we knew it. As one character explained before leaving the East End stated "I fought Hitler for 5 years, only to see the area taken from us, without a bullet being fired".

I expect you think these are extreme views, but be assured they are not, they are the views of the people who have seen the east end of London changed beyond all recognition, although if you utter any words similar to these then you're branded an extremist! Anyone who doesn't conform to the system will find themselves labelled an extremist or a crank, You may not agree with my views on what took place, which ultimately led to the closure of the docks but they are a truthful account of what actually happened, if you don't agree then there is hardly any chance that you will agree with my views on the system. But as the old saying goes "the truth hurts", and believe me this will hurt a lot of people who either held or still hold prominent posts in either the trade union or the government.

Since completing this book I have found myself defending what I have done (writing about what happened in the docks), the code of the Dockers is that we don't talk or tell "outsiders" about our business, this still seems to be the unwritten rule despite the fact that the docks as we knew them are no more. So despite the fact that this book was finished over 6 months ago I have had to rewrite the whole thing again, but this time I have changed the names so as no-one can readily identify the characters, however the story is still a truthful account of both life in the docks and the destruction of the industry.

So I will leave it to the imagination of those who worked in the industry and those whose relations took part in some of the struggles trying to get decent working conditions to work out who's who, instead of being proud of the role that there relation or friend played in making the dock industry a place to be proud of. So I have resorted to naming my characters with non-de –plumes, similar to The Ragged Trousered Philanthropist by Robert Tressill or another classis George Orwell's Animal Farm, before you get out the knife to slaughter me for daring to compare with 2 of history's greatest classics, let me assure everyone the only thing that I liken with the 2 afore mentioned books are the names given to the characters and how things have not changed over the last 80-90 years.

Some Politician's names have also been changed but I don't think that you will have to be blessed with the brains of Einstein to work out who's who. But other politician's names have been left so as they can either sue me or take it on the chin.

The Early Days

I was born and raised in the East End of London ,where almost all of your relations would live in the same street, or if they never lived in the same street then they almost certainly would live within walking distance , as almost no-one owned a motor car and unlike today there were no social services , it was the family who cared for their elderly parents or anyone who were unable to care for themselves , the children would get the shopping whilst your mum would prepare their breakfast or dinner, and this would be repeated 7 days a week, all this on top of running your own home. But it was done not as a chore but as a part of your everyday life. What I do remember from my early days of childhood was that poverty and hardship went hand in hand. The east end of London had taken the lion's share of war damage, and as I was to discover later in life the government of the day expect the working classes to bear the brunt, and be expected to repay the national debt while the big players in life expect to pay almost nothing.

Since writing this book the country has been plunged along with most of the world into a recession, a recession brought about by Bankers, the tax payer has via the government pumped hundreds of BILLIONS of our money in an attempt to shore up the banking system. Fine if they repay it, however it appears that they can continue to pay huge bonuses and still pay shareholders a dividend, leaving the tax payer for the foreseeable future to see their standard of living decline. The politicians seem reluctant to mention this or indeed they don't want to do too much to upset their banking chums, still I suppose with all the revelations about M.Ps expenses it would be the pot calling the kettle black. Ask your local M.P this question, if someone saved your business by pumping huge sums of money into it would you not expect that person owning the business to repay the money before he paid any shareholders a dividend, after all the shareholders would not have a business without the help.

Most of my family worked as dockers and as such if you had sons then they in turn would be expected to follow their father into the Industry by becoming a dockworker, most people in the area looked upon Dockers as being amongst the elite of the industrial workers, this theory was based upon the fact that they earned good wages, well when a docker was at work he did usually have the opportunity to earn good money however, one week at work followed by a week or two without work lays that myth to rest! My father's family were all good east end stock, indeed when my father started work in the Docks he was the third generation of his family to work in the industry, the whole area covering the East End of London relied heavily on the dock industry for their livelihoods'. The list of different industries dependent on the docks would fill a book on its own.

Throughout my life I have attempted to help the working class in their struggle in obtaining a fair deal. I have done this as I have never subscribed to the club "that we are all the same", even today some 30 or 40 years on I believe the gulf is wider than ever, but try and explain this to someone who has just taken a 25 year mortgage and they believe that this makes them paid up members of the middle to upper class brigade! I don't think so. My biggest claim to fame is that despite some tempting offers I never sold out. Employers soon rooted out anyone who they classed as a militant and made them a foreman or a superintendant, whilst the Trade Unions would make you a paid official. Both careers spelt the end of your days trying to put right the wrongs, and, if the truth is to be spoken the person taking the new job was at the start of a new career, that of self preservation.

Today like many thousands of East Enders I have been forced to leave the area that I looked upon as home, with the closure of the docks and all the industries that depended on the docks for a living a new East end has emerged. A new person has emerged ,the professional workers who find the east end a jolly nice place indeed, nice dockside apartments with plenty of wine bars lined up alongside what used to be my place of work. This coupled with the government's policy of allowing mass immigration, many of who settle in the East end making it a rather strange mixture of people, the haves and the have not's, all living happily together- I don't think so!

But while the professional people have all the best homes, dockside apartments, penthouse suites or the best houses in the area the other side of the coin shows that the rest of the population are living on council estates, with crime being the only opportunity for many of the youngsters. Cockney rhyming slang has been replaced at schools with up to ten or twelve different languages. The powers to be wonder why the people have got the right ding dong over the way that they have been treated whilst the folk arriving in the country have been offered housing benefits, social payments and a whole host of benefits. Say anything against what is going on and you are a racist, don't worry about the fact that your children can't obtain social housing, ignore the fact that many young single girls get themselves pregnant so as to get a council home,

Death of the Docks

ignore the fact that many people who have seen the total destruction of their areas and industries are turning to the far right political parties, as they are the only ones listening. Tragically as with many other issues the politicians of all the main parties do too little too late, then they wonder why people don't have much faith in them.

A Way of Life

Wealth doesn't bring you happiness; well this is how the old saying goes, well let me assure you neither does poverty. I believe that this saying must have been put about by the wealthier members of our society to stop the working classes wanting to join their ranks. Show me a man who has no money to feed his family, and then show me a man who is well heeled and wants for nothing and if you can't spot who is the happier of the two then you must be suffering from failing eyesight. Another classic that must have been dreamed up by the same little team is hard work never killed anyone. Its well known that hard strenuous work can put a strain on your heart and that can lead to all sorts of nasty illnesses. Whilst leading a leisurely life does not put these strains on your heart.

In the fifties and the sixties you met both poverty and hardship head on, given the circumstances that you were confronted with in the docks the only way to escape these two evils was to slog your guts out when you got work, this would normally require superhuman efforts and to top it all of this would usually be carried out on an empty stomach. Throw in the deplorable housing conditions and you've got your win treble up, unfortunately you don't qualify for any prizes. No we were all expected to rough it a little after all the war damage plus the financial state of the country. Unless you experienced this then don't even start to comprehend

Death of the Docks

what this was like. Plenty have tried to convince people that they know what the east enders went through because they read about it, they thought that they would through their studies become an authority on socialism and hey presto they would become councillors or M.Ps, these are known as text book socialist, and believe me there are plenty of them about. Given all these adversities you would have had your work cut out to find people moaning about the situation. Today in new labour the text book socialist has been made redundant by the champagne socialist!

What had happened was the war had toughened people up to be able to face up to the most challenging of conditions that society could throw at them, add their humour at being able to turn the tables by laughing at such events and you could see that they belonged to the glass is half full section of society. The humour was still abound, stories that would make front page headlines today because of their tragic consequences', would just be brushed aside with the attitude that someone else must be worse off than me. But faced with all these extremes, it was no wonder that given the opportunity to make an easy few bob on the side, then the temptation often was too great.

Which brings me to the twins, now no book about the east end would be complete without mentioning the Krays? Most of the east end was controlled by the twins and not the police; they had more senior police officers on their payroll than the metropolitan police did. As a result of this they did as they pleased, in the docks all the gates are manned by P.L.A police 24 hours a day and you are questioned and searched if the needs arise, but on this particular day the twins arrived at a shed that had discharged tens of thousands of boxes of apples from New Zealand. Although it was rare for the twins to interfere with the ordinary man in the street they still carried this air of fear about them. They had brought a lorry to the shed with one of their men driving it, they then selected a tally clerk and between them they proceeded to load up their lorry with the apples.

To say that this lorry was overloaded was the understatement of the year; everyone was waiting for the Lorries back axle to go. But it never and the twins just casually enquired to the tally clerk as to where he would be drinking that night ,then they got into their car and escorted it out of the docks. The police just waved then through, that night as promised they arrived at the public house that the tally clerk drank in, as they entered the pub a silence took hold of the bar, they ordered 2 light ales sat down where the tally clerk was drinking, the tally clerk and one of the twins then exited to the men's toilets were the envelope was exchanged and that was that. Lots of books have been written about the twins with varying conclusions, the fact was that crime usually was only committed on their patch with their say so, if a crime had been carried out that may have affected you or a member of your family, then after a quick visit to one of them or one of their minders the culprit usually was given a lesson in where he went wrong.

The twins would later try and repay the shipping companies who they had relieved them of the apples at a later date by offering them their services to end a damaging strike, the shipping companies declined the offer, but the mind boggles at what would have happened had the employers accepted. Shades of the Teamsters union in America?

But generally despite everything, although you could find yourself completely exhausted from the work you may have just done you could find yourself having a cup of tea or a beer and laughing about the incidents that occurred during that day's work. No matter how exhausted or how fed up you may be there was always someone who could have you laughing your head off, the humour was infectious

Death of the Docks

and more often than not the person making everyone laugh was himself in dire straits. There was never a shortage of comedians or someone who could spin a yarn, in fact they were so good at telling you a story you never quite knew whether the story was true or a pack of lies. No matter how outlandish the story may have been you could never dismiss the story, that's how convincing they were!

One such story that I witnessed was an absolute corker, the story teller would always use someone that you knew as the main player in the story, this kind of brought you into the story. A member of our gang was continually arriving for work late, some of the men in the gang were getting fed up with him and started complaining about his behaviour ,the story teller seized the chance with both hands," give him a chance" he stated, he went on to say that the man had plenty of trouble at home. One of the gang states sarcastically what sort of trouble?, no- I don't think it's fair for me to tell you exclaims the story teller, now this is his trump card because everyone wants to know what's going on. Well alright if I tell you what's happened please don't repeat what I've told you, by now you are almost demanding to hear of the man's misfortune. Well he says slowly his son has got his mother in trouble. This brought about gasps of astonishment as anyone getting in trouble could only mean that they were pregnant. This didn't bear thinking about; to get a girl in trouble was bad enough but to get his own mother in trouble! Heads were being shaken and instead of being angry the men were offering any sympathy that they could think of.

When someone asked what the mother proposed doing about it the story teller replied nothing can be done. He then casually informed everyone that the boy had got his mother in trouble by continually eating the father's dinner! The story teller had to quickly take his leave of everyone.

Long before I started work in the docks I noticed that a relation of mine who was an ardent West Ham supporter had stopped going to watch them. Now he tried never to miss a match and even followed them in there away games in London and the south east. When I questioned him as to why he had suddenly stopped following his beloved West Ham he told me that following an F.A cup game at Huddersfield Town on the previous Saturday where West Ham who were in a division above Huddersfield had drawn, the replay was the following Monday afternoon, West Ham were strong favourites to win. I played truant from school that Monday afternoon so as I could see the replay, for my loyalty I got a good hiding from my father when my adventures were discovered, West Ham duly lost the game by 5 goals to 1, this was unbelievable and when my relation was in the local snooker hall the next day he was to discover why West Ham had played so badly. He noticed a senior West Ham player approach the snooker hall owner, who was also the bookie for all the unofficial bets that everyone wanted to place. The player hadn't spotted him, and when the local bookie had paid him a considerable amount of money all hell broke out, the player had betted on the other team to beat West Ham, no more West Ham for him, and he never went to another West Ham game again.

These scenes describe only a tiny fraction of how life was in the east end of London, they cannot begin to describe how everyone mucked in and helped each other out, the way it was viewed was that there problem today could quiet easily be your problem tomorrow, with the beauty of it all was no matter how serious your problem may have been it was sit down and on went the kettle. Within a few minutes you found yourself considerably cheered up, marvellous what a cup of tea can do!

Death of the Docks

This sense of comradeship never left you, if someone else was in trouble you tried to assist. Even when other workers were in trouble you still tried to help them out.

Some years later in the seventies when a company in Plymouth were in trouble they wanted help as they had been on strike for a year and a settlement was no nearer than when they first commenced their action. Now Plymouth isn't just around the corner so we could hardly send a large contingent so we sent 2 delegates, I was one and the other one was later to become mayor of Newham council, the workers who were in dispute worked for an American company called Fine Tubes, they had been sacked primarily for belonging to a trade union, this being par for the course with a lot of our American cousins who thought they could do as they liked over here. We were met at the railway station by the secretary of the sacked workers, he was putting us up for the night as the mass picket was to commence early the next morning. When we arrived at the factory that was to be picketed we were shocked at what was to greet us.

It appeared that the local police responsible for the area had recruited all the policemen who played rugby in the south west and Wales, it seemed that every policeman was about 6feet 6inches, and there did not appear to be a shortage of them. The police who were all rigged out in full riot gear seemed to be spoiling for a fight, add to that that the fringe groups seemed to be in attendance in great numbers and you had a recipe for big trouble. The strikers never stood a chance, they were not street wise when it came to organising demonstrations and marches, we quickly evaluated the situation and even quicker arrived at the conclusion that there was going to be plenty of arrests and plenty of trouble. So with no great desire to get arrested and appear at the local magistrates court only to find that you will be bailed to appear at a later date, so it would mean trips from London to Plymouth on a regular basis until the magistrate decided to punish you. Lo and behold all hell broke out outside the entrance to the factory when the bus carrying the scabs in tried to get into the entrance.

The police were just wading in and pulling out protesters and throwing them into the police wagon, for everyone that they arrested there was 2or 3 bad injuries ,to cap it all some of the students threw a large boulder through the scabs coach window, this was enough for the police, they sent the coach away, scenes of jubilation latest for a minute or two before the police aided with their dogs attacked, snatching the odd demonstrator, but causing plenty of serious injuries, these injuries ranged from broken limbs, serious head wounds to severe bruising. When we retired to the local H.Q in Plymouth it was like a scene from the battlefields in the Boar war. The prospective M.P was a young man named David Owen(now Lord Owen), he had witnessed what had taken place and threats of what he wasn't going to do, and who he was going to contact were flying around like confetti at a wedding. Unfortunately David Owen had his own agenda, and striking workers were not on it.

David Owen and his intellectual friends did more damage to both the labour party and the working class movement when they joined their new liberal party. Their actions split the labour party leaving the coast clear for the conservatives to form the government for many years.

Sometime after the Plymouth trip that I was informed that I had been chosen to give a speech at a South London college, at this time everyone wanted a speaker from the docks at their trade union branch, place of work, public meetings, political gatherings but a college? This was a new one to me. Because of the demand for speakers we had formed a panel from which a speaker could be sent, I was given a piece of paper with a contact name and telephone number on it, on making contact I discovered that the college was Dulwich College, a fee paying school for boys. I was and still am totally opposed to the two tier system of educating our children, why should someone receive a greater quality of education because their parents are rich? But despite my misgivings about the whole thing I reluctantly went ahead with the speaking engagement as the shop stewards had accepted the engagement and had given their word.

What I was not aware of was that my distinct disliking for the education of the privileged had got around the college, also word had reached the principle(headmaster in the school I attended),I was met at the railway station and taken directly to the principles study, after declining a glass of sherry he then set about questioning me with regard to my dislike for fee paying schools, I informed him that our eldest daughter appeared to be gifted ,in fact she was quite clever, I informed him that because I was not caked up with money it was a comprehensive school for her. He retorted by informing me proudly that they operate a scholarship scheme for some boys. We agreed to disagree, he then informed me that the speech that I was about to give was the final part of their union debate, the previous speakers had included Robert Carr, the secretary of state for employment, the general secretary of the T.U.C, the director general of the C.B.I and the national officer for the T.G.W.U docks section. He also informed me that there had been an unprecedented demand for seats, so much so that they had changed the venue for the debate. After such a line up of high powered speakers that had preceded me I was more determined than ever to put our case.

The principle then accompanied me to the hall where all the boys take their lunch, now this was not in my script, as we entered the hall all the boys stood until the principle sat down, I was then given a plate of food. Don't ask me what it was for felt hundreds of eyes watching my every move, this was Tom Browne's schooldays, we were sitting on a raised platform above the lines of tables where the boys were taking their lunch. I quickly apologised for not eating anything as I had a snack earlier. I fully expected a boy to approach the top table with his plate and utter the immortal words, please sir can I have some more? The new venue was the schools chapel, and I was to speak from the pulpit, this was something new to me and probably this will be the closest that I will get to the lord. I was informed that I could speak for 45 minutes and then take questions for 30 minutes, the speech went down well with the boys but not so well with the principle and the teachers. I was informed the following week that the college had been flooded with complaints about a dockworker addressing their sons.

Out Into The Big Wide World

Everyone has one book in them, well that's how the old saying goes, don't you believe a word of it, and how many people in your street have written a book? Anyway writing this book is one thing getting it published will be the greatest challenge since Everest was conquered. If I do manage to get it published then I Hope you will find this book a good read and help you to understand what we went through in trying to keep the dock industry afloat. You won't find any Harry Potters or James Bond characters in this book, but what you will find is that it is full of real life characters. In fact characters' that helped to make the docks a place that was unrivalled for comradeship, humour and dignity.

This is a truthful account of how the system shafted us and led to the closure of the docks. In fact many of you who worked in major industries may find what happened to us was similar to what happened to your Industry. The major difference being that we put up an almighty fight to save the industry. As many of the leading players who took part in our dispute are departing I want to record the events that took place ultimately leading to the imprisonment of 5 London Dockers, followed by the rapid demise of our Industry. Getting the 5 London Dockers released from Pentonville prison must rank as one of the greatest victories the working class has achieved in modern times.

Just stop and ask people why the docks closed and overwhelmingly you will get the same replies ranging from "They were a greedy, lazy lot who were always on strike"- or, "they operated a closed shop", meaning that only their family could get a job in the docks and that they could never get the sack. These opinions were a direct result of the propaganda that the media pedalled to the public on a regular basis, our case was never told to the public. Whilst another train of thought is that the docks closed as a direct result of progress, if ever your employer or your Trade Union attempt to sell you a deal that is a direct result of progress LOOK OUT! Progress for the workforce only means one thing- that more output will be performed with a reduced workforce, which in turn means the Employers make larger profits; this in turn spells the dole queue for many workers who may have helped in building up the company, you will discover later on in the book our employers, the ship-owners developed a conscience, they tried (and eventually succeeded) to convince us that the introduction of modern working methods could only be beneficial to our wellbeing, adding that the old fashioned method of handling cargoes was not good for our health! This certainly was a little rich; Coming from the very people who kept the piece work rates so low that the only way you could earn a decent wage was by slogging your guts out.

The same people also kept the basic wage deliberately low; holiday pay was the basic wage so you got deeper in debt meaning when you did manage to get work all, safety concerns went out of the window, you had to meet your target to get a decent wage, and as a result the accident rate was amongst the highest in all the manual workers Industries. To top it all having created the situation whereby the men stood a good chance of getting killed or badly injured , you then have to survive on fresh air, no sick pay, the ship-owners resisted the trade unions repeated requests for sick pay by stating that sick pay would encourage the men to remain off work longer! I suppose for ship-owners to start worrying about the wellbeing of the registered dockworkers could be compared to the devil throwing a party for people who had done good deeds for lesser mortals. Both of these are highly unlikely.

Yes it was true that we did operate a closed shop, if you wanted to be a docker it was almost a requirement that your father worked in the docks, however, the employers got a small percentage whenever recruitment was made. Again the media "forgot" to report this to the public, but it was generally accepted that if you wanted to get in the docks then the easiest route was via your father(rather similar to the House of Lords)

Dockworkers were most certainly not lazy, if you did not pull your weight then you would receive a lecture from the rest of the gang, as the pay structure was based on "piece work" the less work that you done meant less pay, so there was no room for slackers, if a docker still never heeded the warning and still persisted in not doing his quota of work then that gang would not give any work to that man once that job was finished. It was quiet simple "no work no job". Dockworkers were not greedy; when they got a job it was imperative that they received the correct rates of pay for the job because you never knew when you would get the next job. However, most of our wages were earned as a direct result of the piece work system. The basic wage had been kept deliberately low for decades; this gave the shipping companies and the stevedoring contractors who employed you a guarantee that you had to return a high output every day in order to obtain a decent wage.

So the only way that you could obtain a decent wage was by slogging your guts out, no one outside of our Industry knew this side of the story, all they knew was that Dockers earnt a "fortune". But does it make you a better person if you when you did get work you then worked for "Peanuts"? and as for being unsackable, well again nothing could be further from the truth, there was a whole range of offences that could result in you being summarily dismissed, these were all contained in the rules that governed us, what really got up the employers noses was the fact that they were unable to hire and fire at will.

But the media pressed home the fact that we were the untouchables. If you really want to meet a group of people who fall into the category of being greedy, lazy unsackable and operates a closed shop, then pay a visit to the House of Lords, THIS WILL REALLY OPEN YOUR EYES! And to top it all they vote in their own pay rises every year.

After Hitler had done his best in clearing the east end of all the slums that were called homes, the remaining few that had been spared were in great demand, most streets had more bomb sites (debris) than houses, therefore the few that had remained relatively undamaged had to house the many thousands of east enders who had become homeless as a result of the war. My parents managed to get a basement flat that consisted of one bedroom, a small front room and a scullery (kitchen in today's language) with an outside toilet. Was this the promised land? Or was it one of the "homes fit for heroes" that had been promised after the war. My mother and father were expected to raise 3 children in this hovel, no wonder then that my father spent more time at the housing office trying to get re-housed .Yes these were the good old days. My father's persistence finally paid off when the council gave us a 2 bed roomed house, although it lacked a bathroom and had an outside toilet, this was utopia! Yet despite everything, nearly everyone pulled together and helped each other out in times of trouble.

Death of the Docks

Talking of trouble one dockworker who lived in our street run the Xmas club, this was where the neighbours paid half a crown (12 ½ pence) every week for the whole year, and come Xmas time you had a few bob towards the children's presents and the food, alas the neighbours never knew that the man collecting their money had one or two weaknesses, one of which was that he loved to gamble, and this was where the xmas club money had been invested, unfortunately for the neighbours he had not been blessed with much luck and the xmas club money had gone.He could not confide in anyone, he was as they say" done for", once it was out it was jail for him and even worse the shame brought on his family. He had only "borrowed" the money during the year when there had been no work, his family had to be fed and the temptation to "borrow" some money until the work picked up proved too much , however the work never materialised so he tried having a bet to re-coup the shortfall.

As Xmas approached all the neighbours' were being especially nice to him expecting their payout any day now! He had done a quick tally on the shortfall and to his horror he discovered that he was about £300 short (a fortune then).Something had to be done, the consequences' didn't bear thinking about, to make matters worse there was no work, so while he was taking a stroll through the dock a divine intervention occurred! He spotted a lorry waiting to be unloaded; it had 3 large wooden crates that contained Yardley's perfume, as quick as a flash he grabbed a barrow and gave the driver instructions where to park even though he was not working there, the lorry driver co-operated as he was only too pleased to get unloaded.   The three large crates where for export, he got the first crate on his barrow, the tally clerk ticked it off, then he then went all the way round the shed with the same crate, back past the tally clerk who marked it off as the second crate he then repeated the operation and duly signed the lorry drivers sheet for 3 crates unloaded! Although the lorry driver was a little scared he went along with it, and that very evening the loan club organiser was selling perfume to everyone, you could not buy things like this in the shops then, and everybody wanted some as Xmas presents, the Xmas club was paid out! He informed everyone that he would not be running it again! We also got extra special presents that Xmas. Well they do say export or die! Some 40 years later the television programme east enders attempted to re-enact the Christmas club fiasco, however poor old Arthur Fowler ended up going to jail, perhaps if the B.B.C had done its research properly poor old Arthur may have escaped jail. While on the subject of the television programme east enders the B.B.C must have some strange ideas about east enders as it must be 15 years since anyone laughed.

When I was a child the annual holiday wasn't a fortnight in an exotic location, it was 3 or 4 weeks in the hop fields in Kent. You would pack everything onto a furniture lorry and off you went, for most of us this was an adventure and it was our only experience of the countryside, for most of us we could have been anywhere in the world! You helped during the day by picking the hops and putting them into a large bin, the farmer paid you for however many hops you had picked, so in essence you got paid for your holidays!(I don't think so). Another Xmas and yet again fortune was not smiling on our family after another prolonged period of no work it meant that there was no money for the customary Xmas chicken, after hearing about this another dockworker who lived further down the road nipped over a few fences and took a chicken from a neighbours garden, feathers everywhere but we had a nice Xmas dinner and the chicken never woke us up again! The moral was that you had to look after your family because there was no social security or do gooders helping our cause. When you were really without money, be it through a strike or a prolonged period without work you could call in the assistance board ,these were known as the U.A.B , now this was an experience to end them all, an officer would visit you, list anything that you owned, these items could range from the lino you had on the floor to the wireless or anything that they thought that you could sell, what you normally did when you knew the U.A.B man was coming was to take anything of value next door until he had gone.

One such visit was taking place when the officer smelt the pot of stew that my mum was cooking," that smells nice" states the U. A. B man, my mother informs him that it was a lambs kidney stew , "I have not tasted lambs kidneys for years", my dad never one to miss an opportunity seized the moment with both hands , "would you like to take some kidneys home with you?," ten minutes later after he had filled in a favourable report he left as happy as Larry clutching his lambs kidneys, just as well he never enquired where they had come from .

As things began to settle down I remember that we were one of the first homes to get a television set, everyone wanted to have a look at this new wonder that showed news and live pictures, but the general public took to the idea and so a machine was born that would kill of the art of conversation and the start of gradual brainwashing by the powers to be, if you heard it on the telly then it must be true. In the east end of London the labour party would mop up every seat that was fought, whether it was for the local council elections or a general election. It was said that if labour put up a monkey for election in the east end of London then it would win, I think some of today's politicians are taking that literally. You were brought up with the notion that labour represented the workers while the conservative party stood for people with money, to this very day I have been unable to work out just were the liberal party fit in.

Taking their voting habits over the years I wonder if they know themselves. But this political divide was not unique to the east end it was generally the trend in most industrial cities.

Also most local councillors did the job out of love for whatever their beliefs where, perhaps today's greedy councillors should examine their consciences. Something else that prevailed then that is now missing from our society is respect , at school the teachers word was law, with strict discipline thrown in for good measure, and as for the police well they were feared, even when you had done nothing wrong. To be pulled up and questioned by the police would frighten and worry the life out of you. By now many of you especially the do-gooders, will be tearing your hair out at the very thought that these people who stole anything that they could lay their hands on, well let me assure you that if your family needed food, clothing or coal for the fire then it had to be got.

But before passing judgement, consider the risks they took, if you got caught, more often than not it was off to prison, you lost your job, and as a direct result of both of these punishments your marriage was put under enormous pressures, leading in many cases to a breakup. You most certainly couldn't provide for your family by working one week followed by two weeks without any work. As I stated earlier you had no do-gooders screaming from the rooftops about social injustices or the abstract poverty that existed. You may have noticed by now that I am not a member of the do-gooders fan club, but I will deal with them a little later on! The risks that people had to take just to provide the basic essentials for their family, where enormous, compare this with what goes on today, and has been going on since the days we had an Empire, by the big city merchants and many local government councillors not to mention M.Ps plundering funds from where ever they can, receiving

Death of the Docks

kickbacks, not to feed their families but to satisfy their greed. And if they get caught then they deny all knowledge of any wrongdoing, employ top barristers, leading to more often than not a complete acquittal, that's justice for you. The poor worker had neither the funds nor the ability to engage solicitors or barristers to represent them.

Let me ask you this, who else do you know who gets up to 16 weeks holidays at full pay? Who else do you know who is allowed to buy a second home AND furnish it at the taxpayers' expense, receive full allowance of any interest paid on the second home? And then when they are ready to sell the property they then keep any profit made on the home. The restaurant at their place of work offers you a heavily subsidised top class meal or glass of fine wine, again at the taxpayers' expense. Oh, by the way the pay is in the top drawer league, the list of perks could fill a book, and if you haven't worked out where you can get a job with these conditions, then you could qualify to apply for the job. You don't have to be too bright, or very honest, in fact if you can spin a yarn or two then you're in! Become an M.P.

You may also have detected some bitterness against the system from the writer, well let me assure you that this view was widely shared by the people of the East End, but I suppose if you lived on or beneath the breadline this isn't surprising. The local council finally got around to re-housing us, not because my parents now had four children living in a two bed roomed house, oh no it was because the house we lived in was to be demolished. It felt like we had won the National Lottery! A brand new three bed roomed house, with a bathroom and an inside toilet! What luxuries. No more running outside in the ice and snow to spend a penny. I was now fifteen years of age and I had never experienced having our own bath, usually it was a trip to the local baths on a Sunday morning to have a bath.

With the new house came a front and back garden, most of our neighbours had their gardens turfed, but not my Dad, as this was his first proper garden he wanted it to be something special. So when he was working on a ship that was unloading it's cargo from New Zealand, destiny seemed to step in and give him a helping hand in constructing his garden. Amongst the cargo was a single sack of grass seed that weighed about 100 kilos; however it was not the weight of the sack that aroused suspicions, this was done when the foreman told my father to take the sack to be stored in the lockup. Now you don't store any old things in the lockup, only very valuable cargo or items that the customs want stored away from prying eyes or wandering hands are usually kept in the lockup, so when my Dad was told to put the sack of grass seed into the lockup it sounded alarm bells. Sure enough on closer inspection he discovered that this was not any old grass seed but was destined for one of the Royal gardens, my Dad ensured that the sack was placed inside the lockup but in a spot where he could put his hand through the fence a fill up his tobacco tin 2 or 3 times every day. He would take the grass seed to the cafe where he used to have his breakfast or dinner, where he stored it until he had collected enough.

The lawn turned out to be my Dads pride and joy, I have not seen a lawn to this day that could match the one that he laid, walking on it was like walking on a trampoline, that's how springy the lawn was, and he always thanked her Majesty after the Queens speech on Xmas day! In fact he thought so much of his lawn that during a visit to see my parents after I had got married, I found him merrily watering his lawn, so what I hear you say, the only thing that was wrong was that we were in the middle of a drought and a hosepipe ban was in place, with severe penalties for anyone caught using hosepipes. I said "what are you doing?- you know that no one can use hosepipes".Dont worry son

Death of the Docks

he replied if you believe everything that they tell you, you will end up in a mental hospital, he went on to deliver his reason for ignoring the ban, "if they (the government) got rid of all the illegal immigrants' then there would be plenty of water for the rest of us! Game, Set and match! There was no answer, my father held beliefs that made Alf Garnet a moderate. But whilst he voiced his views aloud they were no different to thousands of others in the East End.

My first job after leaving school was in a grocery store owned by the London Co-op, my wages were three pounds fifteen shillings a week (£3.75). But as soon as I was 16 I decided that I wanted to travel so it was off to Dock Street to join the merchant navy, although my parents were not best pleased about it they gave their consent, 10 weeks hard training at Sharpness in Gloucester and I was ready to conquer the world, this opportunity is not available to today's youth as we no longer have a merchant navy. My travels took me to places you only dreamt about, places such as Pitcairn Islands, Australia, New Zealand, Bermuda, Canada, the U.S.A, Japan, the Caribbean and many other places on the globe. Places I would never have seen, had we had not had a merchant navy; it also helped me to become a stronger person and broadened my outlook on life. But after my last trip had kept me away from home for 13 months I decided enough was enough, and during that shore leave I met a girl who I was later to marry, so that put paid to any more voyages.

I owe everything to my wife, she has suffered my being absent night after night attending meetings, and she has raised our 3 children at times with very little money as a direct result of the wage structure and going on strike trying to rectify it,, never moaned or suggested that I ought to go back to work. We have now been married for over 42 years;

Words could never express my appreciation for the support and loyalty she has given to me.

By now I was approaching my twentieth birthday (you had to be 20 before you could start in the docks), although I still had a few months to wait, I decided to work as a shore gang rigger until then .This job was an arduous and dirty job, the employers also expected you to work a considerable amount of overtime, you would either travel down to Tilbury to board the ship and prepare it for an immediate start once it had docked at the berth it was to discharge its cargo. Your job would then be to get the ships stores on board ready for the next voyage, and to do any rigging that may need doing, the pay was quiet good but the foreman (shore boatswain) thought nothing of approaching you 5 minutes before you were due to finish and "tell" you that you would be working up till 11 o/clock that night. To bad if you had made arrangements to go out that evening, if you refused you were sacked the next day! Everyone was moaning about the working conditions so 2 off us started to organise and get everyone into the trade union, this took us a few weeks and just when we were ready to lay out our demands the shore boatswain was waiting for me as I arrived for work, "Over the office" he boomed, now this was the kiss of death, you knew that this meant the sack.

I reminded him of the last in first out rule, "don't worry I've had to sack 70 men to reach you ". Someone had told them what was going on and they were not going be told what to do by a group of trade unionist, "that will teach you not to play with fire" he seemed to be enjoying every minute of it. I wondered if Queen Victoria was still on the throne. Straight down to the union office expecting support only to be told "there's not a lot we can do". These words seemed to haunt me throughout my life; they did not want to know, here started my first lesson in trade union support, the best deal we could get was that the company (New Zealand Shipping Company) would have to re-engage sacked workers before they could employ fresh labour. Big deal! A few weeks later I got a start date to enter the docks.

THE UNIVERSITY OF LIFE

On entering the docks you were known not by your own name but by your father's name, thus a new dockworker by the name of Joe Wright would be known as Sid Wright's boy, and it took a while before you became known by your own name. You would take not only your father's name but also your father's reputation, so depending on how well known and how well liked he was, the better chance you had of getting a better type of a job. I quickly discovered how you got work, in the Royal Group of Docks every dockworker would all congregate along one side of the Albert Dock Road and the foremen and the ship workers would stand on the opposite side, and at exactly 7.45a.m the call on commenced. But I will cover that later. The shipping companies and the stevedoring companies engaged their labour via the National Dock Labour Board (N.D.L.B), this was who every dockworker worked for. The N.D.L.B scheme was an act of parliament brought in 1946 to give dockworkers some security against the most unscrupulous employers in the country , ship-owners were and still are the robber barons.

It was the ship-owners who deliberately kept down the basic wage so that they could keep the labour strength 2,000 or 3,000 above the normal required levels, thus creating mass out of work conditions when the summer holidays finished and whenever there was a down turn in

Death of the Docks

shipping. The inflated labour strength meant weeks of no work for thousands of dockers, and when I went into the docks in 1965 the basic wage was £11.1.8d (£11.07p)per week, 2 weeks holidays with pay at these rates, no sick or accident pay. But on the bright side, when the docks where bursting at the seams with ships, the ship-owners had plenty of labour to call on and unload their ships.

Some two years before I entered the Docks following a series of strikes and pressure from the T.&G.W.U the Government held an enquiry, this seemed to be the way out for successive governments when they never had the answers as to why the Industry was still working under such atrocious conditions. This enquiry was to be undertaken by Lord Devlin,and his brief was to look at the whole playing field, wages and working conditions that prevailed in the Industry. He reported back about the working conditions and recommended that the Industry be modernised. I might add that this was in 1963 and had you stopped the most pessimistic dockworker and asked how the future might lead to him being thrown out of work, you would have been advised to seek help from the men in white coats!

But let me tell you what the docks meant to the east end of London, the royal group of docks was the largest enclosed docks in the world. Enclosed docks being a group of docks protected by lock gates, to protect the docks against tidal flows, giving the docks a permanent depth of water, thus, protecting the ships against any wild or unseasonal tidal changes. The docks meant employment for many tens of thousands of people other than registered dockworkers; the east end relied on the docks for employment for a whole range of trades, it would be difficult to put an exact figure on it but up to 30,000 different tradesmen &women would have depended on the docks for a living. Although the royal group of docks was the largest it was by no means the only docks in London, you had wharfs and warehouses' stretching all along the River Thames, beginning in the pool of London and reaching as far down as Tilbury. There was the Surrey commercial docks who specialised in importing all types of timber and newsprint, the East India docks, which had been constructed by the east India company to handle the importation of its tea and spice trade.(They would be one of the first to close down their docks. The India and Millwall docks were better known as the West India docks, they handled a whole range of cargoes including the far east trade and the fruits and tomatoes from the Canary Islands. The London docks were primarily responsible for the smaller ships that come from the continent, further up river you had Tilbury docks which would ultimately become one of the forerunners in container handling.

Had you started out by visiting the wharves by Tower Bridge and worked your way down river to Tilbury then you would have witnessed the British Empire without leaving the country, warehouses' full of elephant tusks, or ostrich feathers, giant turtles kept in cold storage for when a state banquet was to be held. Other cold stores would be bursting at the seams with frozen meat, casks of rum by the thousand, tobacco leaves all being sorted to grade ready to forward them to the cigarette factories, in the Surrey docks there would be enough timber and whole tree logs to restock the Brazilian rain forest, and no matter whether the trees were endangered, chop them down, as long as there was a profit. And, the ships would be waiting to berth to bring more! Sheds full of rubber from Malaya, wool from Australia, lambs from New Zealand, beef from the Argentines, tea from Ceylon, and fruit from South Africa and asbestos from Rhodesia. In fact you could go on and on, but it proved in no uncertain terms that the Port of London was the gateway to the world.

Death of the Docks

With all these riches you could be forgiven into thinking that the workers who unloaded and stored such riches would have good working conditions, nothing could be further from the truth, in fact there were no canteens of any description, where ever you where working would be where you had your cup of tea, and one of the gang would have to make it! For your dinner break you would either have brought your own sandwiches or you could go outside to a local cafe. Today the employer would be fined or closed down for allowing such conditions. The washing facilities were non-existent, as for the toilets, well they stunk so much that the fly's boycotted them. No, things had hardly changed for many a year and people seemed surprised when the balloon went up, no; the newspapers and the media never reported this. In truth the dockworkers had drawn the short straw in life, everything had to be performed at such a speed so as the ship could be taken of the berth and begin a new voyage. As the shipping companies repeatedly reminded us" there's no profit while the ships tied up in port", even after the ship had sailed, the cargo that had been discharged into the shed had to be delivered, onto Lorries that would collect the cargo and deliver it to wherever it had to go, this too had to be performed at a breakneck speed, for as the ship-owner would constantly draw to our attention the fact that costs were increasing while the cargo remained in the shed. The demands of the shipping companies were the only thoughts that the employers worried about, as for the welfare or the wellbeing of the dockworker they never gave a dam. Their attitude was just be thankful that we give you a job.

Little wonder then that the accident rate was one of the highest of any Industrial workers, nor was it a big surprise that a dockworker had a tremendous chance of dying between the age of 58 years and62 years, if a dockworker passed this milestone then he had every chance of living to a ripe old age, I might add these statistics are not mine but were supplied to us by the pension trustees when the employers agreed to offer us a pension. In the mean time so many dockworkers were dying and not getting a decent funeral, because they could not afford any life Insurance, or the fact that the employers never had a death benefit scheme, it was left to a group of Dockers to get everyone to pay a shilling (5p) a week, the men who collected this money every week on a strictly voluntary basis.

Over 10,000 men joined the scheme with half of your contribution entered into a prize football competition; the other half of your contribution would go towards paying £75 death benefit to any member who died. This vastly reduced the amount of dockworkers being given "paupers funerals". At least our members would end there days with dignity, to the many volunteers who tirelessly and unselfishly collected the shilling every week, just saying thank you would not be enough. These men should stand head and shoulders above most of us all.

The prime cause for the average age of death for Dockworkers being as low as 58 was, the fact that the industry had the highest rate of accidents and there was no sick pay, and this meant that men would return to before the injury had cleared up, also men who were ill would not take time of off work. Taking this into account, with the little matter of breathing in and swallowing huge amounts of dust, grain, cement, flour or asbestos dust, and many more bags of powders that created huge dust clouds for you to breathe in. This was not beneficial to the wellbeing of your lungs. Some of these commodities would leak dust causing nausea, nose-bleeds, and headaches. Sometimes you would be unlucky and work on a powder or chemical that would cause acute diarrhoea, all this and the putrid state of the

Death of the Docks

toilets it was a miracle that a modern day plague wasn't started.

Another little perk the ship-owner offered you was the opportunity to work in the ships hold discharging meat, the temperature could be minus 10 or15 degrees, absolutely no protective clothing or Industrial footwear, at best you would be given some hessian sacking to wrap around your footwear, this wasn't the ship-owners developing a conscience, it was to keep the meat from gathering dirt from our footwear! Very little protective clothing would be issued, if any at all, so it was hard luck if the bags you were loading or unloading were toxic or hazardous, you just brushed yourself down and took yourself of home, were you would hang your coat up, the rest of your clothes would be washed by your wife and if she was really unlucky she and the kids would be treated to a dusting of asbestos or other toxic powders that dad had brought home on his clothes.

Had Charles Dickens been able to visit the docks in the fifties or the sixties I am sure he would have felt that time had stood still in the docks, and he probably would have penned another novel about the docks, only this time the public would have said that as nothing had changed it was the same as his last book! Despite all of this you knew that you would follow your father into the docks, this was the norm, no different to the mining communities and a whole host of Industries were the son would follow in dad's footsteps. More importantly you were glad of the job and accordingly you never complained about your lot, in fact the docks were a place where you could slog your guts out all day, yet have a laugh about it on the bus going home. It most certainly was the University of Life, it wasn't just another job, this was a way of life, a place that had more characters than the cast of Ben Hur, a place where you could have a good old row with your mate and then share a cup of tea or a pint with him.

Ship-owners were the common enemy, dockers knew the only way to make them listen was by sticking together. Never mind the Army; this was the place that turned boys into men. Men who had morals, no matter how hard up you might have been, you never take of off your own. This is hardly in the ten commandments of today's generation. The comradeship probably stems from the fact that despite the fact that there were over 10,000 men working in the docks, someone always knew who was who, you could find yourself working with your dad, his dad, your brother or your Uncle. I suppose it was a similar gathering that many families encounter at weddings or funerals, but this was at work on a daily basis! A similar scene to that of the House of Lords, with the only difference being that the Docks have gone, while the House of Lords is still entertaining the privileged few on a daily basis.

The nick-name that the shipping companies had acquired was a true reflection on what they were, most dockers referred to them as "THE ROBBER BARONS", never had anyone acquired a name more deservedly. The shipping companies had what they wanted and they were not going to give it up without a fight, and to ensure that their interest would be protected they had the high court judges in their pockets along with most conservative M.Ps, so the odds were stacked against anyone who wanted changes brought in. Speaking of changes every so often the establishment would themselves get embarrassed by the conditions they imposed on dockworkers, so they would get their chums in Parliament to hold an enquiry, this was always a good ploy for buying some time, the men would be told by the Trade Unions that justice would be done, what the trade union

Death of the Docks

conveniently overlooked was that the inquiry would be conducted by some of the employers chums. The amount of enquiries into our industry were held under all types of different disguises, a court of enquiry was one, then you had A royal commission or just a plain report into whatever the problem was at the time, but, the report would be chaired by a high court judge, or better still for the robber barons a Lord from the house of corruption. What chance did we have? And still it went on; we had more enquiries than Frank Sinatra had comeback concerts.

There were 2 main unions in the dock with the Transport& General Workers Union (T.G.W.U) being the largest while the National Amalgamated Stevedores & Dockers Union (N.A.S& D.U) was by far the smaller of the 2 unions, however the 2 Unions were not known by their names, the T.G.W.U was known as the white union whilst the N.A.S & D.U were the blue union, despite the fact the blue union was the smaller of the two it was far more accessible to the men, they never had the amount of committees that the T.G.W.U had and as a result they become far closer to the memberships requirements. The blue union never had the strength that the T.G.W.U had but what's the point of having strength if you don't use it. But whatever union you belonged to did not matter, the fact was that you had to belong to a trade union to go to work, no union card no work.

The closed shop as it was known came in for a lot of criticism from the press, but if I'm not mistaken they operated one themselves! But they never mentioned nothing about this, we realised that unless we all stuck together against the employers then our lot would be even worse.

When I was given my "brief" to start work in the docks I, along with about 20 others who were starting attended a training course, this lasted for 2 weeks and it learnt you next to nothing, what the instructors did emphasise was that you should listen and follow the trade unions, don't follow the unofficial committees . Strange training indeed! Like starting any new job you are nervous, you will have been told by your friends that you are entering "the promised land", it never took you long to realise that if this was "the promised land" then God help those who were sent to the barren land!

You don't have someone taking you round showing you the ropes, what you do get is being told and shown what to do once, after that you are expected to do the job as if you had been doing it for 20 years or so, there was no room for lightweights, if you were lucky your father would take you to work with him but this was probably worse, as he would expect you to do the job as a seasoned professional, and not show him up. Heads you lose Tails I win syndrome! The N.D.L.B 2 weeks training course had shown you how to hook cargo onto the crane, and how to drive a fork lift truck. So you could say that all dockworkers were self taught.

Every job would be a new learning curve as no two jobs were alike, if you worked in a shop or a factory then you knew what every day would bring, not so in the Dock Industry, you never stopped learning the different methods of working. The pecking order for promotion in the docks was quite straight forward, nearly every dockworker would belong to a gang, and each gang had their own ganger, this man would normally be responsible for getting the gang there work, also once at work he would be responsible for the smooth running of the job. The ganger would also liaise between the men in his gang and the foreman, this would depend on whether you worked on the ship or as a quay gang, but both operations had a foreman. The foreman was responsible all the gangs working whatever

Death of the Docks

operation he was in charge of, he in turn was answerable to a superintendant who was in charge of the entire operation. In short the promotion opportunities were zero.

The ship worker or the quay foreman were normally ex dockworkers carefully chosen by the employers, for it was he who was directly in the firing line between the men and the superintendent, he would kid to the men, try to remind them that he was still one of them at heart and most importantly of all the company held him partly responsible for keeping the job going. That would be as high as a dockworker could climb the promotion ladder, for most superintendents were recruited from ships officers who were looking for a shore job, this was the Shipping Companies way of rewarding an officer, many a ships officer must have wondered what they had let themselves in for. For most of them they had spent a lifetime were they had to be addressed as sir, where there word was law, the culture shock for most of them must have been tremendous, dockworkers were not known for showing the more finesse points when an argument was taking place. To see some of the newer superintendents reactions when they were told just what the gang of men thought of them was indeed a sight to behold. Given the tremendous pressure that these foremen worked under it was astonishing that the companies managed to recruit people for the jobs, but the lure of a guaranteed weekly wage in excess of the ordinary dock workers wage seemed too great a temptation to turn down.

As I stated earlier the call on where you got a job would commence at exactly 7.45 a.m, not a minute before or after, however as I was to discover later this was in the main a purely cosmetic routine as 90% of the jobs had already gone, a quick visit to the local tavern at 7 o'clock in the morning would reveal all, the local tavern was called the Connaught tavern, and at seven in the morning it would be packed out, the foremen and the ship workers would go in there and "just happen to bump into the gangers who they preferred to work there ships", a few pints of bitter and 2 or 3 hundred jobs would have been" arranged". Of course they would still have to attend the call to ratify the deal struck in the pub! Other jobs, usually not as good as the ones that had been snapped up in the Connaught pub earlier, would still be available and there was a mighty scramble to get work, dignity went out of the window when it came to getting work, this had been described by Journalist who witnessed it" as nothing short of a cattle market sale", but this was the system and standing back and condemning it would not get you work. There were all kinds of invisible embarkation lines and being a new recruit, who thought he knew it all I managed to get a job myself, no help from my dad or from any of his mates, I felt 10 feet tall, I was as proud as punch!

The euphoria never lasted to long I hadn't gone 50 yards before I got a tap on the shoulder, I went to tell him my good news when he shouted at me "you silly daft B-------, do you know what job you have just picked up?" I told him that I was in a quay gang unloading lambs from New Zealand, this being one of the better jobs, "no son you've just picked up 70,000 cases of butter, and your down the ships hold, you had better phone up Pat (my wife) and tell her to do you mincemeat& mash for dinner because after you've finished tonight you won't have the strength to chew anything! I regret to report he was right, another lesson learned. There is no substitute for experience!

Some days you could go on the call knowing that you had absolutely no chance of a job at all, there could be some three or four thousand men attempting to get one of the two or three hundred jobs that was available that day, men would jostle, push or shove just to get the attention of the ship workers eye, usually without any success.

Death of the Docks

One particular day on the call the ganger was calling of his gang, everyone knew it was a good week's work, and a particular man had just done a week's work with this gang and it had been really hard work for not much money, so this job would level things out. The ganger however would not take this man's book, instead he gave the job to one of his mates, before you knew what was going on the man who had been discarded hit the ganger flush on the chin knocking him out cold, the ganger had dropped all the books into the road so the man who had just knocked out the ganger just threw his book amongst the pile in the road, the ship worker casually bent down to retrieve the books said "that's alright anyone who is desperate enough to knock someone out for a job will do me", and with that everyone marched of as if nothing had happened! But this was no way in which people should have to try and obtain work, this was just another aspect of an industry that was captured in a time warp, something had to give before all hell would break out.

Wild cat strikes were a common occurrence, not an all out dock strike, but a ship would stop work or even an individual gang would knock off, the employers would go on the offensive, not wanting to show any weakness, in would come the Trade Unions, they would listen to your grievance, tell you to go back to work while they pursued your claim with the employer, once they got you back to work your demands would be diluted beyond all recognition from your original claim, and more often than not, the job that was being disputed would almost be completed. But given the atrocious working conditions it was a miracle that there were not more disputes than there was.

To understand the pay system when you went to work you required a degree in advanced mathematics, every gang had their own "lawyer, it would be up to him to study the previous days piece work wages,(this was called the note) every different cargo had a different piece work rate, even then there could be several different rates according to the size or weight of the commodity that you had handled yesterday, then there could be extra money because of the amount of different marks, this entailed extra sorting whereby your earning capacity would be impeded, all very straightforward up to now! Having worked all that out you then got down to the nitty gritty of the piece-work note, say you had discharged 7,000 lambs, if the rate was 15/9d per hundred, you would multiply 15/9d by70 and then divide the total by 13(the amount of men in the gang), add on any awards you might have got and hey presto that's what you earnt yesterday.

Then things get a little tricky when it comes to the guaranteed weekly wage, most workers would take their basic wage and divide it by how ever many days they had to work, not us! To explain it would take up a full chapter, but basically for every day that you did not work you received an attendance allowance, this was called a bomper and you got 80p for each day that you bomped off. now this was now where near one fifth of your basic wage, the logic being that if the employer could find you a job on Thursday or Friday then you would work and lose the guaranteed make up that they had to give you. This would save them money. Because if you had no work for a complete week the N.D.L.B had to "make up your wages", you received 16/- (80p) for every day that you were out of work, but if you had a complete week without work then you received the makeup guarantee, this guaranteed you £11.1.8d per week, so if they could get you a job towards the end of the week it saved them money. So you're confused, if you understand that lot my advice to you is take an advanced Open University course, you'll find it simple.

Such working conditions left an opening as large as a barn door to show resentment towards the employers, the

Death of the Docks

trade unions were long winded in getting changes or dealing with the men's grievances so step forward the liaison committee, these were dock workers elected at a dock gate meeting, the men would instantly recognise these men as one of their own, no minding your language, you said it as you saw it. But as with everything else with the antiquated working agreement the liaison committee members had no powers to settle individual disputes, in fact although they led the actions for better pay and working conditions they still had no negotiating rights at all. Furthermore the liaison committee mass meetings would be held at the dock gates before work, not like the trade unions branch meetings that would take place at 7.30 pm in a school hall after you had done a day's work, so there are no prizes for guessing whose meetings were the best attended, and most important of all the liaison committee attacked the ship-owners and the stevedoring companies, this was music to the men's ears, if there was a grievance then it could be dealt with on the spot, although the liaison committee had no negotiating rights whatever, they certainly made both the trade union and the employers sit up and listen.

The trade unions made it abundantly clear that they never recognised any member of the liaison committee; neither did the employers recognise them as well, but what both the trade unions and the employers never grasped, was that the most important players in the game, were the men, and the liaison committee most certainly did recognise them, in fact the men trusted the liaison committee members implicitly. Had either the ship-owners or the trade unions given the men the respect that they warranted then a great deal of unrest could have been avoided. The main reason for the hatred towards the liaison committee from both the employers and the T.G.W.U, was that nearly all the members of the liaison committee were members of the communist party; the T.G.W.U had banned communist from holding any office in the union and as most communist party members were activists the only way they could represent the men was by serving on unofficial committees such as the liaison committee. This ban on communist party members remained in place until 1968 when the T.G.W.U finally lifted the ban, but by then the damage that the media had done in portraying every communist as agents from Moscow, and hell bent on bringing the capitalist system to an end stuck with the British public.

The newspapers suggestions that communist party members were seeking out key posts in British Industry to cause unrest and help bring about the end of capitalism held no water with the dockworkers. Because the dockworkers were only interested in where that week's wage packet would come from, plots from Moscow would not pay the rent or provide food for their families and, as they never trusted the media or the trade unions they could all go and make love to themselves!

But be under no illusions whatsoever, if you were a member of the liaison committee then your every move would be scrutinised, usually this would be carried out by the countries secret service the M.I 5, no we were not paranoid about this, but it was at the time when the government would have you followed if they thought you were a threat to the national security. In fact before I started work in the docks a famous unofficial leader met with a fatal accident, in many quarters within the dock it is claimed that the man was pushed from a deck in the ships hold and as a result he fell from the top deck in the ships hold to the bottom, killing him outright. To dockers his death was as mysterious as the death of Princess Dianna, or even the scientist Dr Kelly who knew of "the so called weapons of mass destruction "ridiculous or farfetched? Well, you are entitled to your

Death of the Docks

opinion, but I know just what these people are capable off.

However, the liaison committee remained a thorn in the side of both the employers and the trade unions as the men readily identified them as their "own", meaning that they too had to do a day's work to get a living, and that they too would endure the same hardships when there was no work This was the reason that many men did not hold the trade union officials in the same high regard, they looked upon union officials as not understanding our problems as a direct result of the fact that they had a comfortable life style, and believe me there's a lot of logic in that! Another thing that really got the men's back up was the fact that union officials seemed to favour the employers when there was a dispute, for a lot of the men this would be the only time that they would see a trade union official, and what would be there message? "Get back to work", hardly a vote winner was it? But union officials were appointed, not elected so there was no need to worry about not getting re-elected. Once a union official was appointed it was for life.

Armed with this and the terrible working conditions the liaison committee had no trouble in looking for injustices to correct, mass meetings were held on a regular basis with the trade union seemingly doing nothing, usually the chairman of the liaison committee would be a good public speaker, and when I started work in the docks the tradition had been maintained, the chairman was Jack Dash, and could he talk! He could convince you that black was white! He never missed a trick, he would start of by praising the men up, and getting them to believe that they were invincible, he would then launch into a frenzied attack on the shipping companies, and this was music to the men's ears!

It was from Jack that I picked up the art of public speaking, always create a bogey man that the men know, someone the men would love to hate, the more scorn you heaped upon the poor chosen "bogeyman" the better, then just when you have them baying for blood you then switch to praising the men's efforts, you heap the praise to such an extent that the men feel 10 feet tall. Then and only then do you start explaining about the reason for calling the mass meeting, the men by now know that the perpetrator for this dispute was "the bogeyman", while they are the innocent victims. I must add at this point that in 99% of the disputes this was the case.

When the men needed information it would be the liaison committee that would issue leaflets, usually they would be short, sharp and to the point as opposed to the trade unions long and boring leaflets, this was when they bothered issued a leaflet, which was not very often. However as always it was the trade unions that held the whip hand, for it were them and not the liaison committee who would meet with the employers to resolve any disputes. More often than not at a meeting between the employers and the unions that may have been arranged to settle a strike that was unofficial, the first item on the agenda would be to condemn any action that the men might be involved in. The employers would even inform the trade unions that they would only discuss the grievance upon a full resumption of work! The situation beggars belief. How many disputes were prolonged by this ridiculous attitude? The liaison committee were mainly based in the Royal Docks, but the West India docks also formed a committee, add to the fact that other docks and wharves had 1 or 2 men who were interested, so although the unofficial committee never had the network that the trade union had, what they might have lacked in numbers they more than made up with their enthusiasm, to further complicate things the dock Industry was one of the

Death of the Docks

last major Industries not to have shop stewards. So if you had a dispute you or the employer would contact a union official, who would make his way to the berth where the dispute was, this arrangement was far from satisfactory and more often than not led to flare ups.

Taking everything into account it was no wonder that every so often the men revolted and downed tools, usually the stoppage would be unofficial with the liaison committee taking up the mantle on behalf of the men. Given the trade unions inability to be able to deal with problems on the spot or deal with issues that needed addressing immediately, sometimes you stopped work over an issue only to find that it had been doing the rounds in the T.G.W.U maze of committees, it was not uncommon for a resolution to take months in reaching a committee that could deal with it, so the men's patience would be tested to the full. Another ingenious method of settling disputes was for either the employers or the trade union to convene an "area committee", this committee consisted of a trade union official and an employer's representative, with both sides taking turns to chair the proceedings, the men's claims would be presented to the committee and then the employers representative would give his views, the committee would then deliver a ruling that was binding on both parties. More often than not the award was well short of what the original claim had been, leaving the men well cheesed off.

The men would, not unreasonably, stop work thinking that this was the only way that anyone would listen. When the union officials, ship-owners and government departments ran out of excuses they would always resort to the old hardy annual, a court of enquiry, a royal commission a government report usually headed by a Lord who knew nothing about the docks but in all probability he was friends with a couple of ship-owners. We had so many reports and enquiries into our industry it was a wonder that the House of Lords and the high court had enough law lords to conduct their business. If you think that I am exaggerating the situation be my guest and check it out, the classic ruling that came from the court of appeal, it was when asked to rule on a case that defined what was dock work, this had been brought by a company called Parker Packing, they operated in the port of Cardiff, they wanted to employ "non dockworkers" to do our work.

Despite the fact that the case had won the support from the national dock labour board and the high court in London, the appeal court judges found in favour of the employer and in arriving at his ruling stated that "dock work finished when the cargo was unhooked from the ships crane", he had either drunk to much gin or he was finding in favour of the system. In short what he knew about dock work could be fitted on the back of a postage stamp! But the ruling was both dangerous and vindictive, and would be "the law". Another classic was when the government commissioned "The Bristow Report." Bristow was a Q.C, and he was given this nice little earner by being asked to enquire into the dock industry. This report was commissioned by the Government to end a national stoppage, the reason that our wigged wonder was asked to hold an enquiry was to ascertain the definition of just where dock work began and ended, and he was to come up with recommendations for the way forward for the Industry, Mr Bristow Q.C got us no jobs(this was the original claim) for us, but what he did deliver was a proposal to speed up modernisation, or to put it another way the condemned man was told to start constructing his own gallows!

Not for the first time I was having serious doubts as to whether I had done the right thing by starting work in

Death of the Docks

the docks, I seemed to be out of work more often than I was in work, but I could never have envisaged what was waiting round the corner for me and thousands of other dockworkers, for despite all the media coverage ranting on about dockers bringing the country to its knees it was to be the seamen who all but brought down a labour government, as each ship docked the seamen joined the swelling ranks of merchant seamen already on strike, ships where laid up because there were no crews to sign on for the new voyage, A lot of ships were diverted away from Britain to try and avoid the strike. But at the end of the day every port not just London, but every major deep water port was full up with strike hit ships, there was absolutely no prospect of work in the near future.

The government had to devalue the pound, the I.M.F imposed strict monetary conditions in return for the loans they allowed the U.K government. It was at this time I was getting married, my wife to be and I decided to try and buy a house, we found the place we wanted in Essex, a lovely semi detached, two bed roomed house with its own drive, the asking price was a little out of our reach but we decided to go for it, the asking price was £3,995..00, much to our surprise we were accepted by the building society for a mortgage. Although the seaman's strike was official and being led by the union, one of the architects who were instrumental in keeping the strike going was a ships steward, yes- the very same person who later helped to hijack the labour party, renaming it new labour, and then becoming deputy prime minister.

But back to the seaman's strike, not only did the seaman's union help in nearly bringing down the government, but because of the financial restraints imposed upon the country by the I.M.F we lost our house.(along with many more people),the credit squeeze(sounds familiar doesn't it) meant that the building society could only lend us 60%

of the value of the house we wanted, making it impossible for us to proceed. But don't worry, I bear no malice, despite the fact that the house today would sell easily for £300 thousand pounds.

However, put the boot on the other foot and I wonder how senior labour politicians would feel or how they would have reacted to a dispute along the same lines when they had helped previously helped organise damaging strikes to further their careers , now they line up to condemn strikers who may cause unrest through industrial action, it does not bear thinking about.

An overwhelming majority of new labours cabinet have sold their soul to the highest bidders. Morals? They don't have any. Socialism? They can't bring themselves to even utter the word. But canny senior cabinet politicians always had a way with words, and they would have probably claimed that faced with a similar strike they wouldn't panic, on the contrary, our John like Walter Raleigh would have finished his game of bowls, however, bowls being a working class past-time wasn't for our John it would have been a game of croquet. But now that Judas has retired to a life of leisure there are no shortage of candidates' for his job, the only conditions are that you must read and digest George Orwell's Animal Farm, these being the new guidelines for new labour. Ex young communist members, anti apartheid activists, C.N.D members and not forgetting trade union officials, all these are candidates' to become cabinet ministers in new labour, and thereby qualifying them to represent the pigs in animal farm. It justifies the belief that was widely shared by both the liaison committee and the shop stewards movement that most of the fringe groups who showed up at most disputes and demonstrations are today's revolutionaries with an eye on a job in the ruling class tomorrow.

Death of the Docks

Actually what the seamen achieved was no different to what many other groups of "key" workers achieved, the end of your Industry. Once you harm the government that's your lot. The ship owners moved quickly to ensure that they would never again be held to ransom, ships would be registered in faraway places such as Panama and even countries that where landlocked and never had a navy, but this did not matter to the shipping companies indeed it would serve them two fold, firstly they would not have to employ British crews and as a bonus the ships being registered in a country whose income tax was more favourable than Britain's. How many ships sail today under the red duster? Shipping companies who accused us of being "unpatriotic" could qualify for the double standards award.

Following the end of the seaman's strike the docks were empty, the ships were all out of sequence and it would be another several weeks before it settled down with the ships getting back to a normal schedule, I like many thousands of other dockers found myself without work more often than not given the fact that you where rewarded with the grand sum of£11.1.8d a week (before stoppages!) I again wondered if this was the life for me. It was about this time that I met a group of longshoremen (American dockers) who where over here to show us and warn us of the perils of containers, what the Americans had done was to negotiate an agreement to protect their members against mass unemployment that container ships could bring. The deal they had reached with the American port owners was called the M&M agreement, this stood for the mechanisation& modernisation agreement. Now not only had most of us never seen a container ship but many of us had never even clapped eyes on a container.

51

The American trade unionists had secured a deal from their employers that we could only dream about, their employers where no different to ours, they had been told that containerisation did not pose any threat to their livelihood, adding that it would make life a lot easier, removing much of the arduous tasks that were currently required to unload and load cargo by the conventional manner. All of a sudden the ship owners seemed to be developing a conscience, or could it be that they saw bigger profits with containerisation? Many people told me that the little "team" we had met were from the teamsters union, and that they were mafia based. Someone even suggested that if the employer who was doing the negotiations did not agree with the unions spokesman then he would disappear, only to be found floating down a river at a later date. Given on what our respectable trade unions achieved for us I sometimes wonder who represented their members best.

DECASUALISATION

But something was going on behind the scenes that would cause so much trouble that it beggars belief that it was even being thought of, yet alone that it was actually happening. It appeared that secret talks were being held between the port employers and the trade unions to bring about an end to the casual labour system. When I say secret talks I mean secret talks, no-one had an inkling as to what was going on, it emerged later that both sides had entered a pact not to reveal anything about what was being negotiated, the thinking behind this was that this probably was the most important talks ever to be held to decide the industries future, and that as the whole agreement was being negotiated it wouldn't do for the men to hear bits about this and then bits about that. Not that it was our future and that it was our livelihood, this counted for nothing.

Yet again the trade union would show total disregard to the very people who pay the wages for the officials and elect the delegates to represent the views and interests of the dockworkers. Nothing as treacherous had ever taken place, nor would anything ever be allowed to re-occur in the future. But the damage had been done the unions and the employers had drawn up an agreement, trade union officials hailed the talks as the greatest break through by the registered dockworker since the introduction of the N.D.L.B scheme in 1946. The truth of the matter was that both the trade unions and the employers knew that if the men knew what was going on, and what the trade unions were surrendering in the talks, then there wouldn't be any deal. What seemed to have escaped the trade unions attention was the fact that given the disgusting conditions and the poor pay scale that we had, then why should we have to surrender our rule book to obtain working conditions that 95% of the working population already enjoyed.

What followed was almost unbelievable, the trade unions told us what they had done, you almost sensed that they wanted you to congratulate them for bringing the casual labour system to an end, not that this was 40 or 50 years late, not that the basic wage was one of the worst of any industrial workers or the fact that the employers had created a pool of labour over and above normal requirements. Whatever else needed putting right, like the fact that there was no sick pay, death benefit or pension. You never had to have the brains of Einstein to understand what was wrong, but amazingly the employers wanted concessions before giving us what was really ours by right. Even then, when the employers had extracted all the concessions that they could get from the trade unions, there was still no sick pay or any of the other benefits that the majority of British industrial workers already had in there agreements, so what great benefits had the trade unions negotiated for us?

Every registered dockworker was to be given a permanent employer, the basic wage was to be increased from £11.1.8d to£15, still no sick pay only a promise to introduce a pension scheme. What we had to give up to achieve the above was mind boggling, if you had not witnessed it and someone had told you what had happened, you would have struggled to find someone to believe you.

Death of the Docks

The trade unions met the onslaught of criticism and abuse head on, their reaction was one of surprise and anger, the trade unions questioned whether we had the right to criticise their getting rid of the casual scheme that had been a millstone round the dockworkers neck for decades, also they were annoyed that we had not trusted them while the secret talks were being held.

Meanwhile the liaison committee not surprisingly seized on what had taken place, it was almost impossible for them to work out what part of the agreement to discuss, or how the trade unions had conducted themselves, meetings were held several times a week with the attendances increasing at every meeting. The storm clouds were gathering. But despite this there were still many lighter moments, and one of the all time greats when it comes down to being in the premier league of dockland characters.

He was a tally clerk called Dougie Dolittle, he would turn the most serious conversation in howls of laughter with his "one liners", on this particular day there was a shortage of labour, not only for our own dock but Tilbury docks required over 200 men. What this meant was that every man was going to work. Now Dougie Dolittle never got his name by chance, he hardly ever went to work, he worked when it suited him, but generally speaking he would have hardly qualified to enter" worker of the year" contest! After you had attended the "call" to get work, all the men who had not been successful ,would have to go down to the N.D.L.B offices to register for any jobs that still needed filling, or as was more often than not to register attendance, they stamped your work book , this was known as getting a bomper. The jobs that you might get allocated to from there were generally the worst type of jobs, and usually meant that you would not earn much money.

On this particular day everyone was going to work, the N.D.L.B man had told everyone over the tannoy system when calling for everyone to put their work books into the rows of windows that were manned by N.D.L.B officials, these people generally looked down on us; they certainly were not friendly towards us. Everyone was moaning at the thought of having to go to Tilbury to work, this was some 40 miles away, this was further than some of these men went for their holidays! Our Dougie then delivered a broadside "Well I'm not going to work", everyone around him laughed at this remark treating it with contempt, on seeing that they were not taking him seriously he then challenged them, "anyone want a bet?" the men armed with the knowledge that there was no way that anyone could get a bomper piled in ,bets ranging from half a crown up to ten bob were struck. Dougie Dolittle then disappeared for a moment, he reappeared at one of the windows, "could I see the dock manager?" he enquired, as if by fate the dock manger agreed to see him. This was the equivalent of getting an audience with the Pope! Once in his office the manager boomed at him "what do you want to see me for?" very feebly Dolittle produced a football pools copy coupon, "well sir, the men out there keep telling me that I have won a lot of money". The football pools were the equivalent of today's National Lottery, with a top prize of £75,000 an absolute fortune, the manager took the copy coupon and disappeared for a moment. What the manager never knew was that Dougie had filled in a copy coupon after checking the results from the newspaper!

When the dock manager returned to the office he looked visually shaken", go straight home to your wife, you are a very rich man", this was it Dolittle knew he had taken the bait, "but sir, the man at the window said that I was going to go to Tilbury for work today". The manager could hardly hide his excitement, "work" he screamed "you have done your last days work", and with that he took Dougies work

Death of the Docks

book and stamped it with a week's excuses. Mission accomplished! Dolittle returned outside triumphantly where the men paid up their bets once they had seen the proof. However the following week Dougie was summoned back to the window and handed a 4 day suspension! This was hardly a punishment for our Dougie in fact he viewed it as a bonus! Stories like this were common place, the docks were full of Jokers, characters and men who could spin you a story and you would walk away not knowing whether you had been spun a story or whether the man was being serious! To just sit in a dockside café and listen to the banter would give you enough material to write until death us do part and only fools and horses. In fact I am sure that the writers of these comedies did just that to get most of their material.

Back on the work front it was becoming apparent that a strike was almost inevitable, the men where now looking to the unofficial committee for help, the unions had negotiated the deal so it was hardly likely that they would come on board with us in trying to stop the implementation of the deal, the only allies the men had was the unofficial committee. The touch paper was waiting for someone to ignite it. It wasn't if, but when the balloon went up. Meetings where being held almost every day at the dock gate by the liaison committee, So you would leave the dock gate meeting knowing that you would soon be involved in a strike even the trade union called a meeting at the nearby local town hall, but unlike the liaison committee they held their meeting at 7.30 pm, I am sure that they could have held a meeting at the dock gates. They must have known how the men held them in contempt for the capacity of the hall was 600, what would have happened if the entire membership had decided to attend? As it happened only about 150 men showed up and the meeting was a shambles. The day of reckoning was drawing closer. So it was imperative that you went to work to try and get some money behind you, it was because of this that I took a job that I would not normally consider, I took a job that meant that I would be "backing" beef for a week, normally this work would be done by gangs of men who done this job on a regular basis, but obviously they must have been on another job.

Now this was what you called work, although the wages were quite good take it from me that you earned every penny. I must add that the men who performed this job on a regular basis made the job look easy, but to me and the rest of the gang who had taken this job, it was far from easy, in fact I will describe the job to you, I have no doubt that you will be sweating just reading about the job! You had 12 men in your gang, 2 men would unhook the chilled beef from the ships crane, this would now be lowered onto an electric platform truck, another 2 men would drive these, then you had the ganger who would sort out the different marks and tell you what lorry the beef had to go in, so that's 5 jobs gone, leaving 7 men for the remaining jobs, 2 more men would be needed to "lift" each piece of beef onto your back, , leaving 5 men to "back" the beef into the lorries, this was to be my job, the 2 men would lift the hindquarter or forequarter and you would walk underneath as they lowered it onto your back. So far, so good.

Most gangs would be told to do 3,000 pieces of beef for a day's work; each side of beef could weigh twice your body weight. I quickly worked out that 600 pieces of this beef were mine, once the beef was on your back you had to carry it to the lorry it was destined for, also you might have to go up three steps to get into the lorry, once in the lorry you either pitch the beef onto the floor or hang it on hooks in the lorry. At the end of the day's work I knew that once this job was finished I would never again work on chilled beef! In short you were expected to carry twice your body

Death of the Docks

weight placed on your back and be expected to carry it about 35 yards.

One job that I am thankful to this day that I never worked was asbestos, the number of times I witnessed bags of asbestos being discharged with torn or ripped bags, causing the contents to spill out usually all over the men who were unloading it. No masks, no protective clothing just a bottle of milk, this major concession was introduced just before we banned the handling of asbestos, the employer's concession of granting you a pint of milk when you worked asbestos still mystifies me to this day. Did they know something that would prevent asbestosis? Or would the milk just speed up the body's intake of the killer powder. If the truth were to be spoken the ship owners were probably this country's biggest mass murderers. Taking into account the asbestos scandal, whereby we had been kidded for years that it was safe to work, we had become increasingly suspicious about certain unknown powders or dust.

One particular ship some years after we had banned asbestos (far too late), I was called in to a dispute on a ship that had come from Canada to be unloaded in the Royal Victoria Docks, the men had worked unloading paper sacks of a white powder, when they had gone home many of them experienced heavy nose bleeds or sore throats and headaches. I never professed to be a doctor or have a wealth of medical knowledge, but something seemed wrong to me, so I told the men to stop working the cargo, my employer who told me that he always had the men's interest at heart, assured me that the cargo was safe to handle and then proceeded to start shouting about driving work away from the port, when he realised that the cargo was not going to get unloaded he called in the trade unions ,medical experts and the importers of the cargo. I visited the local reference library armed with the details of the substance in question ,and discovered that not only was it highly toxic but under no circumstances should it get near any open cuts or breathed in. Now even with my limited knowledge of the medical profession I knew that working this cargo was not beneficial to your health.

The experts that had been summoned by the employer all assured me that the cargo was safe to handle, I produced a large paper bag full of the powder that I had filled up from one of the bags already in the shed, I then gave them all a teaspoon each and invited them to swallow a couple of spoonfuls each, I was accused of being mad, but I insisted that our men would inhale far more than a couple of teaspoonfuls, and if it was as safe as what they were proclaiming then they had nothing to fear, I added until they swallowed the 2 tea spoonfuls the cargo would remain were it was, the ship was duly taken out with the cargo still on board. This type of dispute was common place, more often than not the cargo would be discharged without any knowledge of what the bags or boxes may have contained.

The trade unions seemed to be playing the role of being the peacemaker more times than not, they saw their role as one of keeping the job working, usually when they were called in to sort out a dispute the men had downed tools, so there first job was to get a commencement of work before they could even begin to try and resolve the dispute between the men and the employers.Little wonder then why the men never had a great deal of faith in the unions, couple this with what they had done by negotiating in secret and their level of popularity had sunken to a new low. As the days passed by the employers and the trade unions carried on implementing the introduction of the decasualisation of the industry, every man was given an employer, new work cards were issued and leaflets' explaining what was to happen on the third Monday in September. Still no-one thought of asking the men if they approved of the deal that had been negotiated on their behalf.

One group who did ask the men if they wanted the deal were the liaison committee, and surprisingly the men told everyone just where they could poke the new deal; however no-one were listening. As the day grew nearer the men voted for an all out strike to commence on the same day as the new deal was to begin. However it was for a higher basic wage and not to throw out the deal that we did not want. Battle lines had been drawn. Every major deep sea Port voted to join in the strike, so although the trade unions were insisting that we continue work and accept the agreement, a national dock strike was due to begin. The trade unions were in a frenzy, they called mass meetings, issued leaflets and the employers even resorted to launching a newspaper, this was called" The Port", and for years it peddled the employers lies and propaganda.

So the strike duly commenced with the trade unions chasing their tails in an effort to get us back to work. What materialised next was mind boggling!, the trade unions desperate to break the strike and get the deal accepted went back to the ship-owners and the port employers, not to re-negotiate the deal but to get another £2 per week on the basic wage, this brought all ports up to £15 per week, London dockworkers would be paid an additional £2 per week in the name of a London weighting allowance. They had pulled the rabbit out of the hat, men voted up and down the country to go back to work, although London and Liverpool voted to continue the stoppage, however in London the only dock who remained solidly behind the strike was the royal docks, Tilbury had gone back so to had most of the West India Docks, although there were pockets of support from men working in these docks the vast majority of the men had returned to work. Coupled with this was the fact that most of London's riverside docks and wharves had also resumed work, the liaison committee knew it was time to call a halt to proceedings, however this would leave Liverpool out on their own, many of our men in the royal group found this a bitter pill to swallow, but the men voted to go back so that was that.

Liverpool were on their own, the trade unions had picked us off port by port, Liverpool sent a delegation down to the royal group of docks in an attempt to get support, but again a close vote saw us not support Liverpool. If the trade unions thought they had beaten us then they had a rude awakening waiting for them, we had barely been back to work a few days when bang, it was of again. We were discovering just what the trade unions had "surrendered" in reaching the decasualisation agreement with the employers. The continuity rule was the most precious rule that was in our agreement, this had gone. What the continuity rule meant to dockers was a protection against being replaced by a gang of blue eyed boys, therefore once you had started work on the ship or the quay the job was yours until the operation was finished. This had gone, so with the trade unions trying to justify why the "crown jewels" had been taken from us we were back out on strike.

We wanted the re-introduction of the continuity rule while the trade unions were telling us that it was impossible to include it in the new agreement, the employers sided in with the trade unions so we appeared to be up the swannee without a paddle. We held marches, we demonstrated in fact we done everything physically possible to try and get a successful outcome to our dispute, and we were knocking our heads against a brick wall. Then the trade union delivered the knockout blow, they got Liverpool back to work, they had been out for the best part of 2 months, Jack Jones had personally intervened and reached a settlement with the Mersey Docks & Harbour Board.

Death of the Docks

It was during this strike that I received what was probably the best piece of advice that I would ever get, the leader of the liaison committee, Jack Dash told me to beware of the press, he went onto explain that the press would slap you on the back today, but tomorrow they would stab you in the back. Never have I received a truer piece of advice.

When you are out on strike the state graciously give a pittance of an award towards keeping your wife and children alive, what happened was that the social security set up emergency offices, they would hire church halls or any large establishment that could cater for thousands of people descending on it in one day, the system was that you took evidence that, if you were married or had dependent children who you were able to claim for, the social security would draft workers in from all over the place to be able to deal with the problem on the spot. The form was that you sat in rows of chairs and waited for your name to be called; you would then be interviewed and assessed as to how much, if anything, you would be awarded. I was awaiting my turn along with my Dad; I asked him why he had bothered to come along as my Mum had a job, meaning he would not get anything."It kills a couple of hours" he told me, I was being interviewed when my father sat next to me to undergo his interview, he had a young girl interviewing him, and when she enquired as to whether my Mum worked, my Dad replied that she did a little job, the young girl then asked to see some wage packets, "no, she gets cash in hand" my Dad informed her. The young girl sensed a killing here, "how much does she get"? She enquired, "about £20 per week" my Dad informed her. She disappeared for a moment and I asked my Dad what he was doing," you'll see" he told me. The young lady returned with fresh forms and told my Dad "we need a few details about what your Wife does and who she works for as it is an offence not to pay Income Tax or National Insurance contributions for employees, she began to complete the form and then asked my Dad what was her occupation, he replied that she did some house work and a little shopping, the girl then asked him if he had the name and address of the person she worked for, "me" boomed out my Dad, the young girl was a little confused," what do you mean" she asked "what I mean dear is she keeps my house clean and tidy and cooks my meals, like you ought to be doing for a man" That was that, the Manager was summoned and my father was told to leave. My Father never bothered to join the political correct club, this never made him a bad person on the contrary he was a very good man.

It was about this time that our leader Jack Dash received a death threat, a threat that the police took very seriously, so much so that they gave him a 24 hour guard and strongly advised him not to address the mass meetings that had been arranged. He refused and carried on knowing that someone who wanted to harm him could be anywhere in the crowd. As stated earlier a very strong rumour that the twins had offered the ship owners a deal to end the strike and this could have been there way of delivering the deal. However nothing happened so I suppose they knew there limitations.

We knew that we were on a loser, the strike had stretched well into November, at one of the meetings that the trade unions had called to try and get us back to work the men, who were getting fed up with the unions attitude all broke into song together, a rendering of I'm dreaming of a white Xmas was served up for the unions! Another nail in our coffin was that the employers had managed to gather enough men who had crossed the picket line to man a ship. Now this was the cardinal sin in the docks, to scab on your

Death of the Docks

brothers was unthinkable, you carried this fatal mistake you may have made to the grave, it was never forgotten or forgiven. If you crossed the picket line then you knew the consequences', a scab takes the bread from striking families and then holds out his hand to accept any rewards that the strike may have achieved.

But for the scabs of 1967 things looked bleak for them, for all the scabs work cards had fallen into some of the strikers hands, not only did the work card show the man's name but in many instances it gave his address and in a few cases the man's telephone number, someone decided to print 5000 leaflets with all the scabs details on the leaflets, the leaflets were distributed at a mass meeting, the repercussions' were enormous, so great that the special branch were called in to track down who had managed to "acquire" the work cards, and to investigate how the work cards had managed to find their way into the hands of the strikers. Many of the scabs rejoined the strike immediately, but the damage was done, for the sake of a couple of days pay they had ruined they entire life. Once a scab always a scab, decent people never crossed the picket line, no matter how hard up you might be. The recriminations were not long in arriving, I was handing out leaflets at one of the liaison committees strike meeting, I went to offer a man a leaflet but before he could take it I saw him falling to the ground, he had been knocked clean out with a single punch to the jaw, the man who delivered the blow said to me he was on the scabs list.

But although deep down we knew we were beat the anger was evident for everyone to see, so much in fact that when the liaison committee recommended that we finish the strike and return to work, the men voted to continue the strike, the bitterness was deeply ingrained in every one of the thousands of dockworkers who were on strike. The liaison committee were shell shocked; this was the first time that anybody could remember of the unofficial committee being "turned over." They quickly made arrangements to visit every major port in the country to try and get support.

I was one of four who were delegated to go to Liverpool, so one late November night we travelled up to Liverpool to attempt to get them to rejoin the strike. The weather that night when we travelled up the motorway was treacherous, the liaison committee had given us £10, this was to cover the cost of petrol in getting to Liverpool and back, also the 4 of us were to have some breakfast after arriving in Liverpool, finally we were told to get some lunch on the way home! Who ever worked out that budget should be Chancellor of the Exchequer! Had we not used our heads by visiting a motorway café on the way up and relieving Rocco Forte who owned most of the motorway service stations of a few items of food we would have starved! In our hearts we knew that our mission was doomed as they had only been back a few days following their long dispute. Because many of the Liverpool Dockers must have felt that everyone had turned their backs on Liverpool, when they wanted support. So what right did we have in asking them for support?

We were met by the chairman of the Liverpool docks unofficial committee Dennis Kelly, a truly wonderful person, who like many Liverpool dockers who said it as they saw it, even though it wasn't what we wanted to hear, Dennis Kelly had a way with words, he knew how disappointed we were, he knew that we sensed that this was the finish, we had know where else to go, this WAS the end. Dennis was like the godfather in Liverpool, he was widely respected by his men, even as we walked along the dockside with him it was as if no-one would walk past him without biding him good morning, he in turn would just nod back. But respect doesn't just appear, it only appears after you have earnt it. When Dennis discovered how low our funds were he accompanied us to his favourite café and told us to have a hearty breakfast, once again Dennis just causally informed the café owner who we were and to give us what we wanted. After a wonderful breakfast he sat down with us and discussed our problems.

Without saying that the men of Liverpool would not feel inclined to come back out on strike we knew, we were done for. He must have seen the bitter disappointment on our faces for he offered to call a meeting of all the ports dockworkers at Liverpool's pier head. It was not worth it Dennis Kelly knew his men and we could have borrowed the world's greatest orator and still we would not have got the result we sought. We travelled back to London knowing that a return to work was the only option open to us. There was still plenty of unfinished business to be performed, the liaison committee had told everyone to go to their trade union branches to remove all the delegates who had been party to the secret negotiations, almost every branch removed any delegates who had been party to the agreement. However the real culprits were the paid officials of the trade union and these had a job for life. They were not elected in the first place and you had no way of getting them removed.

I found myself being elected as a delegate for my branch. But before I could contemplate on what it meant for me we had a small matter of swallowing and returning to work, this was a bitter pill indeed, for despite Jackie Dash's words where he praised us up to the heavens and told us to stand tall and proud, we knew that we had lost heavily.So back we all went to a permanent employer to work an agreement that had more strings than the London philharmonic orchestras string section had. Surprisingly the employers had met secretly and decided to adopt a softly, softly approach, they knew what resentment the men were holding and they did not want any more trouble. Although there was plenty of work it was too late to help us enjoy Xmas, most of us were skint, with no time to try and get a few bob we were all resigned to making do this Xmas.

Just before the strike began my wife gave birth to our first daughter, any funds that we had were quickly absorbed by the expense of such an event. I think that throughout my life I have never known such hardship, in fact had I been stopped by the police I would have been done for vagrancy! So I visited my local bank in the hope of securing a small loan, as our first child had been born just before the strike had started I thought that the bank would view my case sympathetically, all went well with the bank manager and I was set for a small loan, then when he discovered that I was a London docker on strike he immediately asked me to leave, no loan. Informing me that his reason for turning down my request for a loan was based on the fact, that many of his customers, who had businesses, were facing hard times because of the actions of the dockworkers. However as he was showing me out I went straight to the counter and wrote out a pay cash cheque for £25, I assured the cashier that the manager had agreed it and as the cashier had seen me with the bank manager ,and much to my surprise she paid me out! The following day I popped a letter through the banks letter box closing down the account. I never heard a word from them.

The Sting

I had become a trade union delegate at the ripe old age of 22, still as green as grass and wet behind the ears; I was to meet some characters who would sell their mother to the enemy, and still justify what they had done by maintaining she would probably have a better life! They were more slippery than an eel and they could sink to depths unknown to man, but, all the time they are laughing and enjoying themselves convincing everyone that they are doing a wonderful job for the working classes. But all this is hindsight, and what wonderful thing hindsight is. As it was I was pitched in with this lot who, although welcoming me and singing the praises of what I had done, and how things would be different in the future. I might add that these people came across as very genuine people who only had the dockworkers interest at heart. Here I was at the ripe old age of 22, and I thought I knew it all, and if you don't mind, believing that I could change everything. It is my opinion that the next 12 months of my life taught me more about mankind than most people take a lifetime to discover.

Yes welcome aboard the S. S ego trip, and if you are unfortunate enough to get reeled in, then you've had it. This does not just apply to trade union delegates but also to local councillors starting out, at grass roots level everything appears to be perfectly normal, and for a while it is, you may even get 1 or 2 things changed, but usually they would have begun the procedure to reel you in to the system, and it happens without you even noticing! Stage one is to praise you up and make you feel almost indispensable, this goes on for however long it takes for you to believe it. Then they might send you as a delegate to represent the union, stay at a decent hotel, nice food and a decent drink in the evening. You would be told that this is not as grand as some of the trips that they make; being very careful to point out that this is the way to live. Now you may think that you would not succumb to these ploys, well as you don't see them coming and more importantly you actually feel comfortable in the company of people who you believe hold the same beliefs as you. Once they have got your confidence your halfway there. You return home believing most of what they have told you, you're strapped in ready for the voyage on the S.S Ego Trip. Welcome aboard.

Just after we had gone back to work I witnessed one of the funniest moments that I have ever seen, A ship had arrived from Australia and had docked in the Royal Albert Docks, it was to discharge its cargo onto the quay, but before it was allowed to start discharging its cargo it had to unload some 200 gold ingots into a bonded barge to be taken up the river to the Bank of England, as you could imagine the security was red hot with an assortment of watchmen, ships officers, police and customs officers, the gold was in the ships bullion room that was located next to the captain's cabin, moments that I have ever seen, so a journey of 30 yards was overseen by about 50 or 60 men.

Meanwhile we were all waiting on the quay for this operation to finish, and then you could start unloading the cargo, one of men in another gang was going around to everybody to try and borrow 10/=(50p), as he had a reputation of borrowing money and nearly always forgetting to pay back his debts , he was not meeting with much

Death of the Docks

success, he was without doubt a character in the docks, he seemed to be able to charm the money out of you despite the fact that you knew your chances of recovering your cash were almost nil. It appeared that he had drawn a blank in his quest to get "his admission entrance" to the pub. All of a sudden he appeared amongst us all claiming outright victory over us; he then produced from under his clothing a bar of gold! The value of "his" bar of gold would not just buy him a beer but would probably buy him the pub! We knew that it had to go back or all hell would break out, we asked him how he had got it, he told us "I just got in the line and someone gave it to me", he then informed us that he then casually walked down the gangway with it. We had to get it back before it was discovered missing, or everyone working on that ship would have their homes searched by the police that very night. We bought the gold ingot from him for a £1, and we finally, after more trouble than you could ever imagine managed to get it back to its rightful place!

The work was plentiful following the strike and with the employers adopting a softly softly approach trouble seemed a million miles away, however nothing could further from the truth, the employers were scheming and planning there next assault on us, and it was to be the old dockers who would be the next to feel the ship-owners axe .As I explained earlier I had recently been elected onto various trade union committees, nothing to exciting, just minor committees as you would expect for a rookie dockworker who had just joined the ranks of the "we know best brigade", again something very strange was taking place within the T.G.W.U senior committees that governed the docks, delegate after delegate were resigning, citing a whole multitude of excuses ranging from personnel to I can't give the time up to do the job, if this was the case why accept the job in the first place. Anyhow all of a sudden I found myself elevated to the higher committees that covered the dock industry; here I was with seasoned delegates who between them had a lifetime of experience between them. What I never knew was firstly the true reason why the previous delegates had resigned and what was in store for our Industry.

Although most of the senior delegates hated my guts because of my involvement in the last big strike, and my close alignment with the unofficial committee they tried their very best to make me welcome, pointing out that it was the trade unions and not the unofficial committees that had achieved real results for the industry. Although I pointed out that they had been responsible for many cases of non action forcing the men into taking action, and that if they had done their job correctly then there would not have been any need for the unofficial committees. This was not what they wanted to hear, as I was to discover, this, like many senior committees in both the trade union and the labour movement operated a mutual admiration society , or to describe them more accurately they were paid up members of the "my glass is half full" brigade.This is a lovely outlook to hold when all is well, but everything was far from being well, in fact everything was looking decidedly gloomy, so as far as I was concerned the glass was most definitely half empty. Never the less I was repeatedly reminded that I was clever, knowledgeable and a good socialist, on the last point I did not need to be told that by this motley crew, however the cleverness of them in boosting you up helps to remove any barriers that may exist. They actually get you believing that you are a great delegate, what they were saying about me behind my back was a different matter, however if they never had the guts to say it to my face that tells you a lot about them. I felt the same contempt towards them as they probably felt about having me onboard the good ship do nothing. Elderly dockworkers were the next group

Death of the Docks

in the firing line, more revelations would shock even the hardiest and seasoned dockworker, the previous agreement that had seen the introduction of decasualisation was now openly being referred to as Phase 1 of the modernisation agreement for the dock industry. Where there is a phase one there must be a phase two, so if you didn't like the first part of the agreement, what chance was there that the second part would be any better?

The ship-owners and the port employers announced that they would enter talks with a view to introducing a pension scheme. All very good you might think, however before the ink was dry on that paper they then announce that they want every dockworker that was 65 or older to be compulsory retired. Get hold of that lot, if you didn't agree to the new compulsory retirement age then you wouldn't get the pension scheme. Meeting after meeting was being held to get the best possible deal from the employers I reported back to everyone and this was upsetting the rest of the delegates who stated that it showed a lack of professionalism by releasing details of negotiations before the whole package had been finalised. Now they were showing their true colours, I reminded them of their last attempt of being professional cost me and thousands of dockers almost 10 weeks' wages. This was met by giving me a stony look, one that could kill. At least they knew where they stood with me; however it did little to improve relations between them and me.

Looking after the elderly dockworkers was another jewel in the crown that was about to go, at present a docker could work on past his 65th birthday, and many did this by doing light jobs like opening and locking the shed doors, coopering broken boxes or damaged bags, in fact they performed many non-arduous jobs that were essential to keeping the docks moving. Many of them did 2 or 3 days a week, they never earnt a fortune but it got them out meeting their mates, having a beer or two and earning a little pocket money. My Granddad fell into this category, after working for over 40 years in the industry he worked just 2 days a week, it suited him. After taking everything into account that the dock employers never paid any pension, or gave them a lump sum if they retired. You might well have asked why all of a sudden the port employers had the welfare of these men in mind.

The employers first offer was to give all the men who were 65 or older £100 lump sum plus 10/-(50p) per week pension, as most of these men had worked in the Industry for 40 or more years, the offer amounted to nothing short of the greatest insult ever known in British industrial relations. To qualify for the pension the man was required to join the scheme and make just one payment, it would be the pension fund that would then continue to pay the men not the employers. The committee that I was on the no. 1 docks group committee of the T.G.W.U were the body who decided whether it would be accepted or not, this was my first real experience of dealing with high powered delegates. When the delegates reported back on the deal that they and the employers had reached I knew in my mind that this was not a good deal, in fact it stank, however listening to some of the delegates and you would have thought that the deal was our passport to the promised land.

With my limited skills as a delegate I told them that the deal was no good and that the men were entitled to know what was going on, before you knew it they all agreed and suggested that we hold dock gate meetings! This had never happened before; I really thought that this was a turning point. I actually believed that I was making a difference! They were actually going to hold dock gate meetings and inform the men as to what was going on, and, if you don't mind they were going to hold a vote by a show of hands. For these people to go to the members at the dock gate and hold mass meetings could only be described as the biggest climb down ever recalled in the history of industrial relations in the docks. We duly held a mass meeting at the Royal Albert Docks and it was probably the largest ever attended meeting that I have ever seen there, they must have wondered what was going on. I estimated that between 10 and 12 thousand men attended, they were told about what the employers had proposed, the mood of the meeting was very different to how the liaison committee conducted their meetings but at least we were informing the men as to what was going on. All seemed to be going well when the chairman introduced me and plonked the microphone in my hand, now this wasn't in the script, a wave of panic swept over me; I had never done any public speaking yet alone speak to all these men. As I looked down at the crowd it was a sea of faces, I had never witnessed anything like it as I began to talk the words seemed to be not coming out, those words that did manage to escape from my mouth were then booming out of the loudspeakers, an experience that will go to my grave with me. Anyhow I stumbled and mumbled my way through what was the shortest ever speech ever made but seemed to take a lifetime in my mind. My legs were like jelly, and I was sure that I needed the toilet, the first person to get hold of me was Jackie Dash, he put his arm round my shoulder and proceeded to praise me up, other men began to join in and I did not feel so bad, in fact I felt that I had done something for the men and I couldn't wait for the next round!

Jack Dash took me to one side the next morning and offered me advice on public speaking, he told me the cardinal rule was to glance around at the audience just before you were due to speak, look for people who you believe will agree with you, then when you start your speech look at that person and speak as though you were holding a conversation with that person. Moving on to another person when the first person feels embarrassed! I tried this later and it works a treat! When I had recovered my senses after the meeting I challenged the chairman as to why he had done what he did, his reply was that had I known that I was to speak then I would have worried, so home I went to change my underpants safe in the knowledge that I had not had to worry! I knew that this was their way of getting their own back on me for making them more accountable to the men.

Although the no. 1 docks group committee had held dock gate meetings, they appeared to have forgotten that the men expect you to deliver a result after you have taken the trouble to explain everything to them, and why the employers offer had been rejected. This never worried them, they were full of their own importance, and woe betide anyone who questioned there logic, you did so at your own peril. It would appear that "there logic" on the question of retiring of the elderly dockers was one of that they had to go, because the employers would or could not move no to the next part of the modernisation programme until all the over 65s had been retired.

As sure as night follows day I was being continually lectured as to why the "old boys" had to go, and that the modernisation programme could not work with them still on the books. By now I had worked out as to what role these trade union delegates played in the game of life, they were the we know what's best for you brigade. Two more late night meetings were held both on pensions and retiring off the old boys, the second meeting opened my eyes as to what this lot really were about, the employers had offered the same deal but had increased the lump sum to £200, big deal! However as the deal was being discussed by the delegates I found myself in total isolation, I was the only delegate speaking against it, the others had resigned themselves to the fact that although we would like more this was as much as we could get, this would rapidly be followed up by one of the delegates who had negotiated the deal with the employers by informing us that this was a full and final offer, I was the only dissenting voice and as the meeting progressed I was constantly being reminded that being in a position of responsibility held certain responsibilities' and as such that I should think of helping the members instead of continually rejecting offers. Then one of them asked me if I knew of any elderly Dockers who had £200, adding that this was equivalent to approximately 10 to 12 weeks wages for many of them, and they would get this in one go and tax free.

The chairman noting how late it was, said that we had exhausted all avenues and it should be put to the vote. Being the only one who had spoken against the deal and not having succeeded in getting anyone to join with my point of view I decided to support the deal making it a unanimous decision, THEN BAM, the voting was 6 in favour with 3 against. Had I voted against the voting would have been 5 to 4, the chairman told me he would have then cast his vote against leaving it tied, and he then could have used his casting vote. GOTCHA.

I went home feeling ill I never slept a wink. They had done me like a kipper. To this day I have not made a mistake that could approach that one. I went down the docks the next day expecting the worse but I was surprised that it was received without any recriminations. They knew what they were, I still could not bring myself around to their point of view, I had been witness and a leading player in a scene that I never wanted to repeat, and they were far too slippery for me. I had made my mind up that if this was how the trade union carried out its business then I wanted no part of it. My mind had been made up for me, although I never announced anything I knew that as far as the trade union was concerned it was good night Vienna. I resigned from all the trade union committees, this sort of ducking and diving wasn't for me, especially when men's livelihoods' and working conditions are involved. Shop stewards would shortly be introduced in the docks, and this was to be the movement that I would throw myself into.

In the meantime the liaison committee were doing what the men wanted by calling a series of half day lightening strikes, this was to try and get us a decent basic wage, the strikes would catch the employers stone cold, as no-one knew when a strike would be called, only the liaison committee would know when the strike would be called, such impromptu action caused the shipping companies no end of grief ,they would have ordered all the transport to collect the cargo, they also would have started new jobs or ships that were due to finish loading prior to sailing would see their plans go up in smoke. What was hurting them the most was the men's actions on ships that were due to sail, the shipping company would have ordered a pilot, all the tugs and what really hurt them was the fact that they would miss the tide. We had held several of these strikes and the disruption that they were causing gave us hope that we would get the basic wage increased, someone pointed out that the ship-owners seemed to be aware of when the strikes were to be called.

Did the liaison committee have an informer? Probably not, but how then were the employers finding out when the stoppages were being called. The word was put out to find out where the leak was, and in 24 hours we had the answer, the cafe that most of the liaison committee used was owned by an ex-docker, he would let them use the back

Death of the Docks

rooms to hold committee meetings, not only did he let them use the room free of any charges but sometimes he allowed them use of the room after the cafe had closed. The cafe in question was known as the Kremlin,(I leave you to work out why) and on the days that the lightning strikes were held he would be left with stacks of food that he had prepared for that day, so after receiving assurances that no-one would know he would be tipped off on the previous evening so his waste would be minimal ,a ship worker who used his cafe for a cup of tea before starting work, noticed that the display of rolls and sandwiches was almost nonexistent, then a lightning strike would be called .All the ship worker had to do was to visit the café each morning and report back with regards to how many cheese rolls had been prepared! The rest is history, no more tip offs. The café owner had to suffer along with everyone else.

I duly resigned from the trade unions main committees, the dockworkers aged 65 or more were given their bounty's and the N.D.L.B register started to shrink, no more recruitments would be held , this was a danger signal if ever there was one. For me to see the old boys slung out with such a pittance of a payment was not just sad, but as I had been instrumental in allowing it I felt a great deal of remorse. But as always the signals would be put on the back burner by the men as there seemed to be plenty of work, when it comes to the pay packet, tomorrow never comes, not when there is plenty of work today! However as one door closes another one opens and with the introduction of shop stewards I was elected at the company were I worked, this was more in keeping with my beliefs, you are elected at your place of work, you are in contact daily with the men who elected you, and the most important thing was that you receive the same wages as the men you represent.

With the introduction of the shop stewards movement the liaison committee met the shop stewards to hear what their ideas and vision for the Industry was, as most members of the liaison committee had been elected as shop stewards I suppose they already knew the answers before they put the questions! Anyhow the result was that the liaison committee went into "cold storage", the men were informed and the shop stewards movement was born. One of our first duties was to take over the campaign for a better basic wage, and this meant a continuation of the half day lightening strikes. It also meant that we would be in the forefront of the inevitable struggle in trying to keep our work. But the struggle to get a decent basic wage was about to take a completely different route, in our docks the shop stewards had adopted the liaison committees policy, that was a claim for£6 for an 8 hour day or £8 for a 10 hour day(this was for working 2 hours overtime). But the strike had moved up a gear, the shop stewards had begun to link up, and after a lot of ground work by a few shop stewards the results slowly began to emerge, Liverpool, Southampton, Hull, Preston all joined forces with London in helping to form the national port shop stewards committee. Later many more ports would help swell the ranks but for the time being these ports represented a huge percentage of the national labour force.

The strikes were not only on a national footing now but they had been extended to 24 hour strikes, and they were beginning to hurt the employers, also the trade unions were starting to listen, just a little, although they tried very hard to make it clear that they disapproved of the national port shop stewards committee, the trade union had called a national delegates conference to discuss pay. Now, this conference hadn't called a strike since Noah led the animals to safety, its make up suited the unions hierarchy,

Death of the Docks

2 delegates from every port or sector, this meant that the 2 delegates representing London's royal docks could have their vote cancelled out by 2 delegates representing a tiny dock somewhere who might employ 100 men, this was not true democracy, but over the years it had suited the union. To almost everyone's surprise the delegates voted for a national dock strike. Scenes outside Transport House where the delegates had met were similar to scenes when England won the world cup, at last the trade unions were on our side, the beauty of this decision was that they and only they could end the strike. However the fight for a decent wage was now out of our hands, and as I was to discover later the trade unions will accept deals that maybe the members would not. Whatever deal could be reached it would never be put to the members to accept or reject it, the same crew who called the strike had carte blanche to end it without any consultations with the membership. Most disputes that this body called usually ended in tears with a poor settlement.

Jack Jones who was now general secretary of the T.G.W.U had the duty of informing the government that the countries entire docks would cease operating. Quickly a court of enquiry was set up under the chairmanship of Lord Pearson, the committee was to meet both sides, hear the evidence and deliver a decision as quickly as possible. I might add that what the good Lord Pearson knew about the docks could be written on the back of a postage stamp, but that didn't seem to matter. Speed was the order of the day, the countries ports had to be opened up for trade again, the Pearson enquiry team sat over the weekend in an attempt to produce their findings and sure enough in a little over 7 days both the setting up of a royal commission and its findings were completed.

No-one should have been surprised or disappointed with the findings, dockworkers basic wages was to be increased to £20 per week that was it in a nut shell, it had fallen well short of what we were claiming, and as such when the trade union re-convened the docks delegates conference we all expected the findings to be rejected. The government had declared a state of emergency after the T.G.W.U had called its first national dock strike since1926, they could as a result of a national emergency call on 36,000 troops to work in the docks. So although the delegates had voted 48-32 in favour of the national dock strike, many people had thought that the strike would be a prolonged affair, as the shipping companies had declared to anyone who would listen to them, that they would not be held to ransom, so with both sides firmly entrenched, it was a battle of wits, and who would blink first. As far as the dockers were concerned it would be no surrender from them. Once again the union came up trumps; although Lord Pearson and his cronies only delivered a recommended 7% increase on the basic wage the delegates at the T.G.W.U docks conference astounded everyone by voting 51-31 to accept the findings. History has a strange way of repeating itself, on this occasion the award that the union had amounted to an increase of 6d per hour, this was 81 years after one of the docks most famous and historical strikes, the strike in question had been called the dockers tanner strike, a tanner being slang for 6d, and here we were 81 years later being awarded a tanner an hour increase.

There were 47,000 Dockers involved in the dispute. The newspapers had banner headlines the next day proclaiming that dockworkers had broken through the sound barrier! They duly reported that we had achieved a basic wage of £20 per week and that other industrial workers would be lining up to follow suit. What they never reported was the disgusting response that all dockers felt; we knew that we had been sold done the river. But what was gratifying to know was that the national port shop stewards committee had arrived, not only had they arrived but the unions, the ship owners, the port employers and the government knew that here was a group who truly represented the men, and the only group who would control them were the men. We were about to enter the most crucial stage of any change in the entire history of the docks. As you will see we tried at all times to take the trade unions with us, however you make up your minds as to why they declined to assist us at the very crucial stages of our dispute. The national port shop stewards would meet nationally about once a month, generally in Birmingham (this being central for most ports) however as the dispute over re-claiming our work grew, we met almost regularly on a weekly basis, add to this that we would have to report back to the London shop stewards and to the men, life was one round of meetings.

THE NATIONAL PORT SHOP STEWARDS

The problem that was attacking us was containerisation, a few container depots had sprung up outside the docks whereby labour was being recruited (usually non Union) to load and unload the containers, we knew that this was dock work but in a different name. It appeared that the problem was not unique to London; most of the other ports were witnessing the same experience. Under the Act of Parliament that had set up the N.D.L.B scheme, any work that was thought to be dock work would be investigated, if the work was deemed to be dock work the owner of the establishment would then be notified, and he would then have to apply to join the N.D.L.B scheme.

All very simple and straight forward, however the container bases were outside the docks and therefore their owners ignored any such rulings from the N.D.L.B This meant that the N.D.L.B had to take the employers to court, not that that was our only problem, some of these container bases were seeking clarification on whether the work that they were carrying out was dock work at all. The trade unions told us not to get too excited as they supported our claim and that right was right. We, unlike the trade unions held out no expectations at all from either the judicial system or from politicians, we had already had a ruling from a drunken law lord defining that dock work ceased being dock work

Death of the Docks

when the cargo was unhooked from the crane, he must have been on the lash because no sober minded person could come up with such a ruling. But a ruling is a ruling, and the drunken law lord had set our cause back light years. Even the government were embarrassed by this ruling and in an attempt to appease both the trade unions and the entire dock labour force they set up yet another parliamentary enquiry, this one was to be headed by a Q.C ,Judge Bristow was to lead a team to define what was and what was not dock work. They took evidence from everyone who had a vested interest in the clarification of dock work and just as important, where the boundaries should end.

We held little or no hope at all on the outcome of the Bristow report, but yet again because the trade unions had participated with the enquiry we had to wait for the findings. Despite all this going on the men were not entirely sold on the subject of the threat of containerisation, the docks were full of ships and there was hardly any talk of redundancies. Another threat that was beginning to appear was the introduction of non-scheme ports, these were ports outside the N.D.L.B scheme, and they could claim a big advantage over ports that belonged to the scheme, as the employers using labour under the N.D.L.B scheme had to pay a levy based on the man's earnings, this helped to maintain and run the local N.D.L.B , whereas the ports that where outside the scheme had a distinct advantage over the ports inside the scheme as they paid no levy, Felixstowe and Dover were the 2 best known ports operating outside the scheme, however smaller docks were beginning to appear, something had to be done. But valuable time was being lost while the judicial system and the government enquiries all took place.

Jack Jones who was now the general secretary of the T.G.W.U was being portrayed by the media as a staunch left winger, along with Hughie Scanlon of the engineers union they were being portrayed as the terrible twins! Jack Jones certainly had his moments, and after following a succession of right wing general secretary's he was indeed a breath of fresh air. However history will show that in his endless pursuit of recruiting members he overlooked the first rule of expanding any business, never let go of the foundation that built the business in the beginning, and it just happens that it was the dockworkers whose membership and their contributions help build the T.G.W.U into the giant it had become.

Dear old Jack in his endless pursuit for new members allowed and actively encouraged the recruitment of the men who were working in the container bases doing our work. The obsession for members that Jack Jones and the executive council shared would come back and haunt us, when some years later we looked to the T.G.W.U for backing, who they would back is now history, as they had both sets of workers as members their decision would not be straight forward, as it would have been had Jack Jones listened to us and had not recruited the men working in disputed container bases, we continually asked the question to the general secretary if he thought it was right by recruiting members at places (Container bases) that we were right fully claiming as dock work. His reply never wavered, "If they don't join the T.G.W.U some other trade union will sign them up, also every worker has the right to be represented" Another thing that had also emerged from the Pearson enquiry was that "the modernisation programme should be speeded up", talks between the unions and the employers began in earnest, and this time however they would be conducted in "an open goldfish bowl" basis. At least they had learned their lesson on that subject.

The N.D.L.B had begun court proceedings against container base owners who were refusing to comply with the decisions that had been taken under the act of Parliament that covered the docks, as for the contents of the Bristow report recommending that all container bases within one mile of the river, should be inside the national dock labour scheme and as such should employ registered dock labour, well this report had sunk faster than the Titanic, so it was up to the courts, the union told us not to worry because the law courts had to rule under British law, and, the law was on our side. How they kept a straight face when telling this to us I will never know. Time was not to be the only obstacle in the way of the unions, as everyone knows high courts and courts of appeals are not known for being speedy. But the trade unions who received delegations of shop stewards on several occasions assured us that they were confident of a successful outcome THERE GLASS WAS DEFENITLY HALF FULL.

The national port shop stewards committee held absolutely no faith in the British legal system, they had never ruled in our favour and we didn't think that they were about to change the habit of a lifetime now. But we had to let the trade unions go through the procedure that was in place to settle grievances', the first high court ruling found in our favour! Don't get too excited, because the ink wasn't dry on the court's ruling before the employers lodged an appeal to the court of appeal. While all this was taking place we also had another sideshow taking place, talks on introducing the second stage of the modernisation plan were really hotting up, and the employers were desperate not to see a repetition of another dispute that heralded in the last change in working practises. It appeared that most local grievances that warranted the intervention of the shop stewards were being settled up by the employers without too much resistance. Most claims were being paid in full, something alien to port employers, but they wanted peace at any price.

The unions and the employers reached some sort of settlement on a new deal, it was to be known as Phase 2 of the modernisation programme, the weekly wage would go up to £34 per week, the hours worked would be reduced to 35 hours less your lunch break, brand new amenity blocks would be built on top of all the warehouse sheds for the men to enjoy their lunch, and an added luxury was that brand new toilets would be built (such luxuries), full sick and holiday pay. The agreement was to be hailed as a forerunner in industrial agreements, it was on the surface an agreement to end them all, the icing on the cake was the total abolition of piece work, you received the basic wage whether you unloaded one ton or one thousand tons, and also there was no bonus system at all, and you received the full wage whether you worked or not. However all that glitters is not gold, this was a really good description of the proposed agreement, on unravelling the agreement every rule or rights that we had left were to be swept aside, there would be nothing left at all, manning was gone, employers had the right to move you about as they saw fit, all these new proposals were alien to the registered dockworker The trade union were very confident that it would be eagerly accepted.

A minority of shop stewards who were against the deal had leaflets printed pointing out the pitfalls. I am proud to state that I was the instigator behind this move to get the scheme thrown out; it never made me to popular with other shop stewards and delegates who had negotiated this deal. But I knew that if you gave up every working practise that had taken a lifetime to achieve then you had absolutely nothing to bargain with when it comes to achieving a wage rise.   When the voting papers were counted it showed a clear majority against the deal. To say that the unions

Death of the Docks

were shocked would be the understatement of year; the employers were as stunned just as much as the unions. Those of us who had campaigned against the deal began to have hope that democracy was really alive and well. Both the trade unions and the employers quickly reassembled the committee that had come up with the package, and quicker than Tommy Cooper pulled a rabbit out of a hat they increased the basic wage by another £2 per week, not only did they get this but they pulled out all the stops in getting the men to accept the new deal. This time they called meetings, produced leaflets whilst the employers used the port newspaper to itemise everything good about the document. Even Jack Jones became involved in getting a yes vote, he personally issued a statement that read "for the first time in the history of the docks the dockworker has a decent deal, a high guaranteed wage, job security and for the first time ever a deal that would enable dockworkers to be able to secure a mortgage", this was all too much for the men to resist, the intervention of the general secretary was too much for the no lobbyist to overcome.

It was overwhelmingly accepted by the men on the second secret ballot. Jack Jones would rue the day that he ever uttered the words" that for the first time in the history of the docks every registered man can safely go out and get a mortgage". Never the less the employers had with the introduction of two shifts split the labour force in half, had extended the hours that work could be carried out, but they had taken an enormous risk in removing any incentives. They along with the trade union delegates who had negotiated the deal believed that the dockworkers would continue to work flat out for the same pay, when in fact they only needed to do a fraction of the work that they were required to do in the past, tonnages plummeted, and the men were going home more refreshed than when they started!   The docks seemed an eerie place too many people, the docks had been robbed of its vibrancy and the buzz was missing, it seemed that they were deserted; you could walk along the rows of sheds and hardly see anyone. Now you might ask why the employers agreed to such a deal when even the dimmest person could have worked out what would happen, human nature would tell you that if you pay a worker £10 a day regardless of whatever the tonnage is done , the worker is not going to break any world records!

Several other important things were going on at this time, gradually we began to see the return of the temporary unattached pool, this being as a direct result of the speeding up of closures from London dock right the way down to the West India docks, many of the men had worked at small wharves along the river, when along came groups of asset strippers, these were people who would buy the wharf, close it down, then sell it off at a huge profit for development. Decent people, I think not. One of the largest groups of asset strippers was a company called Slater Walker, these being Jim Slater and Peter Walker, it just so happened that Peter Walker was a cabinet minister But he made it quite clear that he had relinquished any dealings with the company. Believe that if you want to. Prime Minister Edward Heath and his cabinet had picked up the remnants' of Barbara Castles attempt to handcuff the trade unions with the failed legislation In place of strife. They introduced all kinds of new anti-union laws; the centre piece of the legislation was to be a court that would oversee the new anti-union laws. Despite several large mass demonstrations against the bill it became law. What the government didn't propose was a law to stop asset strippers.

The T.U.C who had helped organise the demonstrations found themselves and their member unions directly in the firing line. What happened next was that despite the general council instructing all member unions not to register with

Death of the Docks

the new court many did, the new court was to be based in London's Chancery lane. It would have powers to impose huge fines on the trade unions for carrying out any form of industrial action against employers, even if the action was unofficial it still did not matter, once the employer had sought an injunction against the workers who were taking the action, the trade union who represented the workers were deemed responsible, even if they disassociated themselves from the action, they would be held responsible. Huge fines would be imposed on any trade union whose members had ignored the courts. Now this was a law that guaranteed big trouble.The trade unions saw this as a threat to their very existence, and to add to their worries the T.U.C s instruction not to register or recognise the court left them very vulnerable. The court was to be run by a high court judge by the name of John Donaldson, he was better known in his own circles as black John Donaldson. We thought of him as a modern day hanging judge, if he had the powers I am sure the man would have either have transported you to the colonies or better still sent you to the gallows.

The court of appeals overturned the high court's ruling giving us the right to man container bases, still the T.G.W.U tried to keep the lid on events by informing us that an appeal was to be lodged to take the ruling to the House of Lords. How they kept a straight face while they were telling us this I will never know, we had absolutely no chance of the good Lords backing the dockworkers claims. Bearing in mind that one of their Peers was a very large employer of registered dockworkers, and it was he, who was to lead the fight against dockworkers claiming work at container bases.

We had a problem and it was not going away, in fact it was growing bigger and bigger as every month passed, so with the legal arguments almost exhausted it would fall on to the national port shop stewards committee to do something about it. They set about carrying out a complete investigation into the ownerships of any container bases within the vicinity of your port. We began to step up the amount of meetings we held, various methods of dealing with the problem were discussed, however industrial action was the very last resort to be considered, as we believed that we could meet with local port employers and convince them that this work could be carried out within the confines of the docks. Not surprisingly most of the employers would not go along with this Idea, although in London at a later date the P.L.A set up a company in the Royal Victoria Docks to load and unload containers, a small victory but unless the shipping companies gave this venture there support the whole venture would be pointless.

The shop stewards inquiries found that many of the container bases set up outside the docks were in fact owned by shipping companies and port employers, some of the shipping companies involved in the conspiracy included the Blue Star Line, the Glen Line, Blue funnel line, Cunard, Shaw Savil Line, Ben Line, New Zealand shipping Company and many many more, in fact nearly all of the major ship-owners had their fingers in the pie, not to be outdone you then had the existing port employers who currently employed registered dockworkers. They had decided that if they were to have a future in cargo handling then it was not with registered dock workers. Many of them had invested huge sums of money in these container bases, money that they had earned by employing dockworkers to load and unload their ships, so the theory that goes "the harder you work the more secure your job is" had been shot to pieces by the employers. The fact was the harder you worked, the more profit the employer could invest into a venture that would put you out of work. So gradually the scene was taking shape, the government had not just moved the goalposts but they had nailed them up with plywood, their colleagues the

Death of the Docks

shipping companies had got the government to introduce laws to stop any resistance against the methods they had planned.

The new court in Chancery Lane had already dished out huge fines to a couple of unions for action being taken by their members, although the action against the employers bringing the "lawsuits" was unofficial action and was not with the consent of the trade unions, this had the other trade unions running for cover .Any possible chance that we had however remote, of the trade unions leading the fight to reclaim our work had just disappeared up the swannee with the introduction of the anti trade union court. Black John Donaldson was on the rampage. Hold on tight, the goings going to get tough so the time to get out was now, there would be no room for the faint hearted, the T.G.W.U made last ditch efforts to get solutions to our problems, they also warned us that any action that we might propose could spell the end of the union.Our reply to Jack Jones was simple, A series of one day national strikes were held, these like most of the action being organised were being led by the national port shop stewards committee, and feelings amongst dockers were running high, we felt that with the re-emergence of a pool of labour that was surplus to the employers requirements, we were rapidly returning to the bad old days. As if this wasn't bad enough the pool of unwanted labour suffered wages cuts making life very difficult. This was not what progress and modernisation was supposed to bring us, we had in a matter of a year or two returned to the haves and the have not system. The strikes were a success; yet again the ship-owners and the government had been embarrassed as a direct result of how the modernisation plan was backfiring.

Yet another committee was formed to rectify the mistakes of the previous committees, this one was to be known as the Aldington/Jones committee, Lord Aldington was the chairman of the Port of London Authority while Jack Jones was the general secretary of the T.G.W, U The committee was to investigate and find a solution to the problems that our industry was facing. Like so many previous committees who had enquired or investigated into our Industry before, this committee would prove to be no different; their solution was to allocate all the men on the unattached register to employers who by their own reckoning already had enough labour. Then to introduce a voluntary severance scheme, men who were approaching retirement age could apply for the payment of £1800. If ever a scam was hatched better, then I would like to know. The beauty of this scheme cried the perpetrators' was that these men could not earn this money even if they worked right up to their retirement age. Those who were against the scheme would stand accused of taking money from our old boys. Ingenious.

They had papered over the cracks, as it was this would be the last chance that the "so-called experts" would have of sorting the problem once and for all. In defence of the trade union delegates who represented us on this committee, you can only achieve agreement if both sides want to reach a deal. But the trade unions should be protecting their member's livelihoods', it should be the main priority of the trade unions to be able to see what the future holds, but our trade union appeared to be blind. The port employers and the shipping companies knew what plans they had in store for the future of the Industry, so there was no chance that they were going to agree to something that would scupper their plans. They had got everyone to work for the time being, as someone took the severance pay that man would be replaced by one of the dockworkers from the unattached pool.

Death of the Docks

Peace had been bought for a few more months; yes we really were beginning to reap the rewards of modernisation! Up to now our benefits read as follows= the total closures of the Pool of London,(this also includes Tooley Street, Hays Wharf and every other wharf that could either be demolished or converted in luxury riverside apartments). We had witnessed the demise of the Surrey Commercial Docks, the East India Docks plus the West India Docks (you may know these docks today as Canary Wharf), Regents Canal had gone along with many more smaller docks and wharves that had served London for over a century, the labour force had been halved, ships were being turned around far quicker with the introduction of fork lift trucks and palletisation. The only benefit that we were getting was the social security benefit. Another myth that came with modernisation was the story being pedalled by the media was that the housewife would benefit from modernisation; yes the housewife would see prices fall as a direct result of savings made through modernisation! Yes the media reported that importers would pass on any savings made thereby bringing down prices. So who was benefitting from the changes? How many households saw prices falling? I fear not very many.

Lord Vestey is a name that springs to mind as one of the main beneficiaries' from containerisation, dear old Sam owned everything that he touched, Sam and his family owned the cattle ranches in Argentina, they obviously owned all the cattle, and the abattoirs plus the transport company that carried the chilled beef to the docks in Buena Aeries ,where the dockers who loaded the beef into the ships hold also worked for the good Lord. With the beef safely aboard a Blue Star ship, which incidentally he also happened to own. Once alongside in London or Liverpool the whole operation would be repeated by the Vestey empire, again he owned the stevedoring company, the road haulage firm that would transport the beef from the docks to the cold storage depots, from there it would be distributed to the nationwide chain of Dewhurst butchers shops, yes you've guessed it, he owned them to!

His chain of companies must have given a torrid time for his accountant's. For when they returned the yearly profit on which Vesteys companies were taxed virtually nothing was earned! Leaving Sam to pay virtually no income tax! Yes this is not a misprint the Vestey Empire paid very little tax for the whole year. There was a rumour doing the rounds that the company had only paid 10p tax. I don't believe that as we all know that Lord Vestey is a pillar of English society.

One rule for the rich? Don't you believe a word of it. Despite the Vestey fortunes seemingly taking a turn for the worse it did not interfere with his ability in purchasing racehorses or buying polo ponies, nor did it seem to interfere with his close relationship with the Royal Family. Yes, if you needed to save a bob or two Sam was your man for a few tips! The stevedoring company that he owned in London was called Thames Stevedoring; it was based in London's Royal Group of Docks and employed some 600 men.

Another stevedoring company in London was T. Wallis Ltd, the company was owned by Tom Wallis and his sister, the company had stevedoring operations in every major dock in London, his company in the Royal Docks employed some 600 men at its peak. I worked here and became chairman of the shop stewards committee on the introduction of shop stewards, the company was made up by ordinary shares that Tom Wallis and his sister owned. The shares were £1 shares and every year they treated themselves to a dividend of £1.50 per share. Not bad eh? Where could you invest a pound and receive £ 1.50p every year with your original pound still intact?

Death of the Docks

You might be beginning to understand now why we referred to the employers as robber barons. In fact what had happened since the turn of the century was the stevedoring companies had earnt fantastic amounts of money, this being due to the fact that the basic wage was low and many stevedoring contractors had no liability after the labour force had loaded or unloaded their ship. The responsibility of the entire labour force was left to the N.D.L.B, not a bad little set up for the shipping companies and the stevedoring contractors-eh?The national port shop stewards had aired many views in an attempt to reclaim our work, one view that had been under discussion was for our members to refuse to load any containers that had come from container bases, we had to dismiss this idea because it was almost impossible to find out accurately where the container had come from. Another idea that was under serious discussion was for an all out stoppage in an attempt the bring matters to an head, however whilst not dismissing the idea it was put on the back burner, a strike would be the last roll of the dice, we had to find other ways of beating the rogue employers. Along with all the other major ports we regularly held mass meetings to keep the men informed of any moves.

This was our trump card over both the employers' and the trade unions both of whom subscribe to the leave it well alone and hope that it goes away club. The simple fact was that it was not going to go away ,if anything the cancer that was destroying our industry was close to being diagnosed as terminal, and if it was not treated then the end would come very quickly.

One idea that was gaining support amongst the Shop Stewards was to identify particular container bases, put pickets outside the container base and hope that the lorry drivers would not cross our picket line. Shop stewards from all the ports took this idea back to their committees to consider the merits of it; the general principle of this scheme was accepted with a proviso, what would happen if all the lorry drivers went through our picket line? Whilst all this was being discussed some of the men along with some of the shop stewards began visiting the container bases that might be considered to be picketed, we had to establish how many entrances there were, how many lorries use the base each day and how many people worked in the depot . The eagerness of the men willing to help us was a good point, they knew that the bases would have to be picketed over a long period and that there would not be any easy victories.

Let me explain to the people who thought that we were just claiming the work to save our own skins. A container is a part of the Ships furniture and fittings, the container with its cargo inside it would be loaded into the Ships hold. No-one could dispute that the contents of a container was cargo, and, no-one could dispute that the loading and unloading of ships cargo was dock work. The introduction of container bases to do our work was no different to you shopping at your local shop every week, and then discovering that the counter were you are served had been moved back a little with new assistants replacing the very people who had served you for years. The men never cared about how long they were expected to picket, this put the tin lid on it, for you can have all the bright ideas in the world, but if you don't have the troops with you then you're done for.

What really put the fire into the bellies of our men was about the same time as we were observing these depots I received a telephone call from the trade union, it appeared the Trade Unions research department had discovered that one of these container bases in Stratford was owned by my employer, we went to visit it, he (Tom Wallis) had really pulled the rabbit out of the hat this time, the location was in Stratford, East London, about 3miles from the docks,

Death of the Docks

the company was called London(East)I.C.D, the I.C.D representing inland clearing depot.The premises were on the site of an old British Railway workshop and railway yards. The company was part of the container giant O.C.L, dear old Tom had joined the big boys league! Despite the dilapidated condition of the site it was obvious that huge amounts of money had been spent, also more money was required to be invested as the site had bonded warehouses and as such the whole area had to be secure. The site was known locally as Chobham Farm. I returned to the dock and requested a meeting with the directors of our company in the dock, Tom Wallis was furious, he claimed the whole thing was an invasion of his privacy, what business was it of ours to pry into his affairs, what he chose to do with his money was of no concern of ours, furthermore the work in his dock companies would not be affected by his new venture.

This was what we were up against, the patronising, condescending and outright liars. This was who you were dealing with, but most annoying of all was the fact that they treated you as an idiot, and challenged your integrity. But it was the trade unions who were pulling their hair out, as the court set up to control the unions had opened for business, and sure enough they were handing out huge fines, it was like taking candy from a baby as the unions had decided not to recognise the court and as such the cases against them were being heard without anyone representing the unions, not that it mattered as the whole court was set up against the trade union movement. Yes, black Jacks court was holding a grand opening, however there was no grand sale to mark the occasion, just black Jack helping himself to the unions funds.

Several huge demonstrations had been held against the anti trade union laws being introduced , with the main players of the demonstrations being the print workers, their unions organised the rallies with guest speakers from the left wing section of the labour Party (not Barbara Castle), all the marches would have bands playing rousing music, in fact most of the demonstrations became a grand day out, very little, if any trouble occurred during or after the protests .But the conservative party argued that they were only doing what the labour party had attempted to do, they were not going to climb down like the labour government. Indeed it was trade union bashing season, and everyone wanted a piece of the action.It was about this time that the national port shop stewards came up with a corker, what if our members picketed the container bases that we selected, requested the lorry driver not to cross the picket line as the men inside the container base were doing dock work, if the lorry driver after hearing this, then crossed the picket line then details of his company would duly be noted, and a nationwide ban would be imposed on every one of that companies lorries in every major dock. Furthermore the company would remain on the blacklist until such times as a letter on that company's notepaper, and signed by one of the directors stating that none of their Lorries would cross our picket lines before they would be removed from the blacklist. Each port would select their own container bases to be picketed with the emphasise on ensuring that the container base could be picketed constantly, it would be no good if it fizzled out, this would be the end before we had begun. Also each port would supply each other with a list of any haulage firms who had crossed our picket line, lists would be upgraded each day so that any firm who had crossed the line would know their fate instantly.

Privately we had one huge reservation about this scheme, and that was if the lorry drivers just ignored us and crossed the line in their droves', then the scheme would be almost impossible to operate. The list that would contain the names of the haulage companies that crossed our picket

Death of the Docks

line would come to be known as the "cherry blossom list" But while we had our concerns about the size of the list we knew that the haulage firms also would have concerns. But as no-one else was either doing anything to rectify the problem or indeed even listening to us this was a gamble we had to take. Furthermore despite any reservations that we may have had this was the best idea that anyone had come up with to eradicate the problem. Each port had to take the details back to their own shop stewards first and then to mass meetings of the men to get the policy endorsed, this most certainly was not difficult, but I suppose you could liken it to asking the condemned man if he would like a stay of execution or even a pardon! The difficult part would be making all the arrangements of ensuring pickets would be there both regular and in numbers, and making sure the "cherry blossom" list was distributed daily. Then there was the small matter of making sure our members did not unload or load a lorry that was on the list.

The next part of the scheme was to select what container bases to picket, these would be chosen with care, the final list that was put to both the shop stewards and the men , the companies that had been chosen, showed a definite link of port employers who had either employed registered dock labour in the past, or had existing links with the docks by employing registered dock workers.

First on London's list was our old mate Lord Vestey, he owned midland cold storage, as the name tells you it was a cold storage warehouse based in Hackney, East London. Then we chose Chobham farm who as you know was partly (49%) owned by Tom Wallis, he at present employed about 1100 registered dockworkers throughout the Port of London. This container base was in Stratford East London, and it was only half a mile from midland cold storage, and its closeness would be handy if there was ever trouble. Both of these places were only a short bus ride from the docks, and in many cases they were closer from the homes of our members than the docks were.Last on the list was a container depot based in Dagenham, Essex it was called Hays Transport, it was again owned by the hays wharf group who had closed down their dock operations at hays wharf, discarding the men who had worked for them over many years. So the dye was cast, we were about to enter the arena for the fight of our lives. Although there were only 3 container depots on London's list the size of the list that they were drawn from showed that the cancer had really taken hold of our Industry and it required urgent attention.

The trade unions were not sure of what to make of us, they had let us down by going down the legal road, in fact over the last 3 years while all court cases and legal stuff was taking place they had not got us a single job in any of the container bases. They could not accuse us of not giving them a chance. Also this was the period when the problem had really taken a hold on our industry, had we nipped the problem in the bud some 2/3 years ago then the struggle would have been a lot easier. Both the trade unions, and, strangely enough the national dock labour boards had used the British legal system right up to the House of Lords, I say strangely because all the dock labour boards are made up equally by port employers and trade union delegates, given that it was the port employers who were operating these container bases with outside labour, they must have been mighty confident that the courts would rule in their favour! Ask yourself would you invest in something with a small fortune and then join a protest group to stop it? Or was it that they knew that the outcome would favour them?

The national port shop stewards committee had done all the leg work on behalf of their members, it was usually the same people who travelled up to Birmingham most Saturdays, the other ports were in the same boat as us with

Death of the Docks

the same people attending week after week, sometimes a different shop steward appeared but in the main it was the same shop stewards who met in Birmingham, a couple of times we travelled to Birmingham only to discover that due to the lack of attendance we could not hold a meeting, if this didn't deter you then you knew you were dedicated. No-one took much notice in the beginning of a" bunch of crackpots who had nothing better to do with their time". However as time went on they began to sit up and take notice, after we had a series of one day strikes other ports contacted us to let us know that they supported us and they would be sending someone to our next meeting. The media was rolled out with all its might, once that they had established that we meant business they went into overdrive, "communist controlled" was the order of the day, and when they took the trouble to interview our "leaders", they never quoted the actual statements that were made. More often than not they would take the scissors to the interview, and come up with something totally different to what was said.

People wondered why we never took kindly to the newspapers and the television, as for the medias slur that we were being controlled by communists, well the official trade union had more communist in office than what we did now that the ban on them had been removed. I would pay the highest tribute to the "mainstays" of the national port shop stewards committee; they were the unsung heroes for giving up their time, effort and expertise in the quest to correct one of this countries gravest mistakes' they never expected rewards, publicity or accolades for the relentless effort they put in week after week, month after month in their attempt to reclaim our work, the only reward any of these men ever wanted was our work back.

Let Battle Commence

We knew that when we commenced the picketing of the container bases that we would have vast numbers of our men turning up for picket duty, at the start of the campaign this would be a novelty for many of our members, it would be up to us to ensure that the novelty did not wear off. All we needed to do was to ensure a regular stream of pickets turned up at their designated container base, we had surveyed these bases closely, and never found any problems like nearby amenities where the pickets could get a cup of tea or a beer. We had explained to the men that it was important that no depot should ever be left without pickets, as it turned out the men done us and themselves proud, some of our men would spend more time picketing the container bases than they spent at home. We never knew how long the campaign would last, this was unchartered territory for us, but what we did know was the campaign would not be over quickly, and that it would probably turn ugly.

Out of fairness to the workers who were already working in the bases we decided to ask to meet there representative or the work force. The object being to explain that we were not out to get them the sack, and to explain to them that the work that they were doing was our work. In fact at chobham farm I was part of the team that met there rep, we informed

Death of the Docks

him that the container base where he worked was to be picketed, adding that if they joined forces with us we would do everything in our power to see that the men working there became registered dockworkers. This was too much for them to take in, they did not believe us when we said that we would get them made up as dockworkers, the fatal mistake they then made was to go to the employers and ask them what they should do. No prizes for guessing what advice they received, the employers called in the police (I don't know why) then the trade unions, the local trade union officer never knew what had happened, I assume he must have contacted head office, he seemed to disappear faster than he appeared, along came a docks trade union officer demanding to know "what the hell do you think you're doing"? The answers he received would not be printable, however I am sure he knew and so did the person who sent him, know what sort of reception he would get. The real purpose of his visit was to get a shop steward to phone transport house and speak to Jack Jones. One of the problems that the t &g w u had was the both sets of workers were union members' belonging to the same Union, we had warned the union of this and for the union it was stand up and be counted time or get the hell out of it.

We were not shocked by the workers response to our olive branch, the wages they were receiving was a pittance for the work they were expected to do, the conditions also left a great deal to be desired. We were disappointed in them turning to their employer for advice; a great deal of hurt and animosity could have been avoided had they trusted us and not turned to their employers for advice. One group who did believe that we meant what we said were the lorry drivers, at first they didn't know how to react to us; some of them did not think that we had the right to picket somewhere we didn't work. (As did 99% of the population), But all in all we were quiet pleased with the initial response from the lorry drivers. However those lorry drivers who had taken cargo in through the picket lines had to be shown that we meant business.Many of the lorry drivers did not know what to do, we advised them to contact their bosses before crossing the picket line, but some of them just drove through thinking nothing would come of it. What in fact did come of it was the picket would phone a number they had been given to report any lorries that crossed the line, this was the "cherry blossom" office, somebody would be on call to take the details, then they would be passed on to Liverpool shop stewards who would add it to their list before phoning it through to Hull where the whole exercise would be repeated, they would then phone the next port, so in a matter of 30 minutes the whole exercise would be completed. We had organised the whole thing like a military operation, every shop steward had a role to play, this made the shop stewards who normally never got heavily involved feel important and it worked a treat, shop stewards who were used to the "Hardcore" doing most of the work couldn't do enough to help, in fact we found ourselves with very little to do as a result of our new found assistants!

Many of the larger haulage firms who were on the "cherry blossom" list believed nothing would happen, how right they were, nothing did happen when their Lorries turned up at the Docks. The men were magnificent, they turned away lorry after lorry, and the shop stewards office was a hive of activity. The transport managers of the haulage firms who were on our list were phoning up to get their company removed from the list, they were informed that for their company to be removed from our list we required a signed letter, stating that there company would not cross our picket line again this letter was to be signed by a director of the company, and it was to be on company headed paper.

Death of the Docks

They were then told that the letter could be delivered to the shop stewards office or the picket line, until then they would remain on our list, and as such their haulage company would remain blacked in every port in the country. The response we got was amazing, they flooded down to the docks with their letters and we had won round one!

We had fully expected our employers to put our men of pay for refusing to load or unload the lorries on the blacklist, for some unexplained reason this never happened. To this day I am at a loss in trying to work out why the port employers never removed men from pay for refusing to load or unload lorries that were on our blacklist. What we had achieved in only a few days was amazing, but we knew that we were in it for the duration, however a little success does wonders for the morale. The Fleet Street hacks were at it, bully boys, blackmailers you name it and they portrayed us as the evil demons of the working class movement, they printed stories that the prime minister would later use in Parliament, stories that made Alice in Wonderland seem like real life. What we were being accused of was setting up shop outside small businessmen's premises and bullying him and the labour force into submission. No attempt whatsoever was made to get an accurate view from our side, but as we were used to this sort of treatment it didn't worry us unduly, we had a job to do and we intended to do it. The general public were being spun a whole load of untruths and it would get worse as we got more successful, we stood accused of driving small businessmen out of business, and of attempting to get innocent workers the sack so as we could then take their jobs. Hardly impartial reporting was it?

It was then that a haulage firm in Liverpool took the T.G.W.U to the national industrial relations court in Chancery Lane, the union unable to defend themselves under the T.U.C policy was fined £50,000 plus penalties to be imposed on a daily basis while the action continued. Now as the T&G.W.U were not doing a thing to harm this company they thought it unfair, so after consulting the T.U.C the Unions were allowed to be represented in the court by a solicitor or a barrister.

Black John Donaldson was having none of it, Perry Mason could have appeared for the T&G.W.U, he would have lost his first case, for despite employing the finest legal brains available, Black John after hearing the legal arguments put forward, he caned them for another £30,000, he was having none of it! The T&G.W.U were reeling from the judgment, how could they be held responsible when the action was being taken without the unions support, or even indeed against union policy. They wondered if one of their members committed a murder would the union be held responsible by the court in Chancery Lane.

Meanwhile on the picket line outside chobham farm writs began to appear from the national industrial relations court, bailiffs began to serve the writs instructing you to cease picketing. The writs were served against no-one in particular but against various shop stewards committees, if you moved you were served with one! Strangely enough this did not seem to be stopping anyone from picketing, Back at Chancery Lane Donaldson heard that the trade unions might run out of cash,(many trade unions had removed their money from the banks and sent it overseas), he told them not to worry about being short of cash because the court had the powers to seize any property that the trade union may own. Ouch! The trade unions didn't know what way to turn, some of them registered with the new court, this was required under the legislation but was in direct contravention of the T.U.C. policy, never before in the history of the working class movement had such a direct attack been made on the movement.

Death of the Docks

What the conservative party and the anti-trade union court never realised was that by upsetting some of the big players in the Trade Union movement, they had removed any chance of most of the unions registering, and thereby in due course recognising the Court. No trade union delegate would be seen dead in Chancery Lane yet alone in Big Black John Donaldson's court. Undeterred Black John instructed the court bailiffs' to issue the writs to the shop stewards who sat on the committee, the bailiffs were asking the men as to who were the shop stewards, can you imagine the run around the men give them? One person who they pointed out as a leading light on the shop stewards committee was about to be served with a writ when the man decided to "go for a walk", the bailiff followed him to try and serve the writ, the man who was not a shop steward then walked for a couple of miles, the bailiff was now convinced he had his prey, chased him in an attempt to stop him and serve the writ, the man would gradually let the bailiff catch him before increasing his pace, after some while the man retired to the pub, the bailiff came running in and proudly declared "I here-by serve this writ on you, as you are a member of the shop stewards committee", every one burst out laughing before informing him that the man was not a shop steward. The bailiffs must have reported back to Donaldson at their failure to serve writs onto shop stewards, so it was back to the drawing board for dear old black Jack and his jolly band of swagmen from Chancery Lane. Two weeks into the dispute and we were well on top, most of the depots were almost empty, we had not expected such gains so quickly, the lorry drivers would not cross our picket line, in fact if their bosses asked them to go to one of the container bases that was being picketed, then the lorry never set out at all knowing it would be futile. But we knew that we had to maintain a presence outside the bases for if we slipped up now then all the good work would be for nothing.

Southern Stevedoring Company announced that they were to cease trading and return their labour force to the N.D.L.B for re-allocation, during the press announcement put out they frequently made reference to the labour force, how loyal and hard working they had been, adding that there had been no other alternative open to them, the press statement was very conservative with truths and the crocodile tears shed regarding the labour force carried no weight at all amongst the men in the docks. Some 1,250 men were to be returned to the N.D.L.B, this was nothing short of a catastrophe not just for the industry but for the men and their families, there income had just been halved at a stroke. Modernisation had paid yet another visit to 1,250 dockworkers and their families.

Southern Stevedoring Company was a holding company for a number of shipping companies, generally they traded with the Orient, but they also handled vast quantities of tea from India and Ceylon (as it was known then),the shipping companies who owned southern stevedoring included The glen line shipping company, blue funnel shipping company, furness withy group and amongst others the British India shipping company, a motley crew in anyone's language, these were the undisputed champions of the robber barons league. What southern stevedoring had chosen to forget to report was the small matter of a container group that these shipping companies had formed to do the work that had previously been done by the men of southern stevedoring.   The company was called O.C.L it had been formed to handle the new container trade, they had joined forces with Tom Wallis and hey presto Chobham Farm was conceived! This container base was only one of a huge network of container bases up and down the country, vast sums of money had been pumped into the venture, money I might add that the registered dockworker had helped them make, but the company had not made any provisions to

Death of the Docks

include them in their modernisation programme. Lots of the men who were to be made redundant had worked for the company for 25 or30 years, and in other cases even longer, the remaining employers left in the dock cried enough is enough. Not only had southern stevedoring dumped 1250 men onto the already swollen pool of labour that who were deemed to be "surplus to requirements", but the vast number of ships that had plied there trade had disappeared without a trace, you could say that we had a modern day Marie Celeste, the only difference was that this time a complete fleet of ships had disappeared the crew of 1,250 was safe and sound and being cared for by the N.D.L.B.

The remaining port employers could see that there was a chance that they would be forced to absorb the men discarded by southern stevedoring, so as a protective measure against such a thing happening they all declared to the local N.D.L.B that they too had a surplus of labour. The whole exercise had been arranged with military precision, It was imperative that something was done to counter this audacious move, the trade unions made all the right noises but were found wanting when it come to direct action, probably because of both that the men who had been engaged to work in these container bases were members of the T&G.W.U, and the ongoing threat of huge fines from the court in Chancery Lane. The union seemed more concerned as to where we would picket next, as indeed were the communist party; this being the last thing on our minds as we still had a job to do at the three bases that we were picketing.

Two weeks into the dispute and we found ourselves well on top, most of the premises that we were picketing were empty, I.T.N news done a special broadcast from inside Chobham Farm it was like a huge empty aircraft hangar, as people spoke their voices echoed, but we had kept up the pressure, one of our daily checks was to telephone the manager of the container base acting as an importer wanting to use his base, or impersonating the press, asking how they were coping. Not once did we get rumbled, in fact on one such enquiry they told us" that they (Chobham Farm) had devised a plan to beat the pickets outside their container base", we could hardly believe what we were being told! They had worked out a programme to résumé handling cargo, they then told us "we will send unmarked lorries to Wanstead Flats(a nearby group of fields) and transfer the cargo from the haulage companies lorries onto our own lorries, then onwards to Chobham Farm ",the manager went on "dockers are a lazy lot so we will do the switch at 6a.m , long before they get up, by the time they start picketing the whole operation will be done and the pickets will know nothing about what has gone on " The following morning long before 6 a.m we turned up to greet the lorries and the workers from the container base, the lorry drivers duly returned to their depot, with the cargo, leaving the workers and the management trying to establish who had informed the other side. They become obsessed that someone within their ranks was informing us. They never found out how we were discovering their moves. We even sent in one of our men as a reporter covering the dispute, once the management heard our man slagging of the dockers they opened up, showing him the empty warehouses' citing that normally these would be bursting at the seams, when asked how they intended to resolve the standoff they launched into us and finished by triumphantly proclaiming "we will never employ dockworkers."

Lord Sam Vestey was attracting attention that he did not need, when asked why he had set up these operations outside the docks when there were plenty of cold storage facilities inside the docks he bumbled "the cold stores that we require are very modern", when asked why he did not employ registered dockworkers he quickly went

Death of the Docks

on the defence "I would gladly consider as to employing any registered dockworker –once they have taken their severance pay! Thanks a bunch Sam. Back at Chancery Lane the barristers acting for the T&G.W.U must have caught Black John on a good day; they had successfully argued that the members who were engaged in the actions outside were acting in defiance to the trade union policy, adding that they were doing everything in their powers to stop the unlawful action. The court accepted their argument; the T&G.W.U were off the hook! What a relief, indeed they had not told the court any untruths for they did nothing to help us in our quest to regain our work. Realising that the men inside the container base were members of the T&G.W.U, and as such the union owed them as much loyalty as they did us, we decided to meet with them again, we told them again that we did not want to get them the sack, and if they joined with us we would ensure that they became at the very least on par with our wages and conditions, ask yourself this question, what would you do in similar circumstances? Your wages would be doubled, your hours of work would be less and you would have better working conditions.

Anyhow once again they decided to report it to the employer and ask him what they should do, not a wise move, but each unto their own. What the employers did get from the representative off the workers was names of people who met them and of people on the picket lines. The other container bases in the area where getting very jittery that they could be next on the list to be picketed, and they started contributing to fighting funds to fight us legally if we turned up. Nice to be wanted isn't it? By now the whole media was in a frenzy, and demanding that something be done to stop this unlawful action-nothing about how many thousands of jobs we had lost,- nothing about the fact that most of these container bases were wholly or partly owned by the same people who where sacking us. They were beginning to sound desperate, and many of us began to scent victory, we even started planning were to go next.

The first breakthrough come when Barking container base applied to the N.D.L.B to join the scheme and thereby engage registered dock labour. We expected a flood of applications to follow but it was not in the script of the national association of port employers.Oh no this was not to be the norm. Quickly regrouping, the container base employers got the representative at Chobham Farm to name 3 shop stewards who were involved in the action outside the container base where he worked, he only knew one, someone he had recognised from his school days, yes he remembered that he went to school with Alan Williams, this was enough for them, they threw in the chairman's name, Vic Turner plus the secretaries name Bernie Steers and they were in business again. The whole dispute was about to change.

A writ was issued and duly served, not without the bailiff's life almost meeting a sudden end, but we were informed that the court tipstaff would seek their arrest on that Friday. The national port shop stewards called for an all out strike to commence on Friday. Ports who had not previously attended our meetings got in touch to inform us that they would join the strike on Friday. What actually was to take place was that the three named shop stewards had to appear in court at Chancery Lane to answer the writs that Black John Donaldson had issued, even the biggest optimist on the planet must have known that there was more chance of finding roast pork on the menu at the local synagogue than the three dockers attending the national industrial relations court.

The easiest thing for the three named shop stewards to do would have been to attend the national industrial relations court and adhere to the writ- that is to cease picketing,

Death of the Docks

and to cease encouraging others to picket Chobham Farm. They could quiet easily have been replaced by others on the shop stewards committee. But unlike the trade unions we chose to stand up and fight,history has proven that appeasement only delays the inevitable. Non attendance would be deemed that they were in contempt of court, and as such could be imprisoned, the general council of both the T.U.C and the T&G.W.U met and it was a close run thing as to who won the prize for issuing the best statement with most hot air yet still declaring an unconditional surrender. The T& G.W.U did make us an offer of letting the men have use of their barrister; this was a magnificent offer especially as two of the three men were members of the blue union! Not surprisingly the offer was turned down. The media decided that all their big guns should be covering this event as it had all the hallmarks of a top story that would run and run. It was the journalist who informed us that Donaldson had issued the warrants for the arrest of our three men; We made arrangements for the families of the men to be given protection from the press and to collect their wives and families to visit their husbands in Prison should the inevitable happen.

Every Port was at the ready, as Thursday arrived there was no change in both camps, it was agreed at our mass meeting that we would all attend Chobham Farm on Friday to give our men a rousing send off! The T.&G.W.U were getting frantic about reaching a settlement, again they offered us the use of their barrister, but this time the brains in the union had come up with a devious plan, let the barrister say sorry to the court, and give the hanging judge of Chancery Lane an undertaking that none of the three men would ever picket Chobham Farm again! They went on; you could interchange your pickets daily and elect a new chairman and secretary, this would throw the court into confusion. Now we knew why we paid union dues! They weren't interested in us, they just wanted to save their own faces.

Friday morning and efforts were still being made by the powers to be to avert the impending disaster, one that most certainly was not our making. The newspapers that day had pictures of the three men plastered across their front pages, with lots more about the three men inside, who they were, anything that was printable with one glaring omission, not one newspaper carried any stories about why the three shop stewards were prepared to go to prison, our struggle to get our jobs back had gone right out of the window. The general view being peddled by the newspapers was that the three men weren't interested in anything other than becoming martyrs. We did not introduce laws that could lead to trade unionists being put in prison for attempting to keep their jobs.

It was a lovely sunny day outside Chobham Farm, and as the morning wore on the crowd began to swell, the container base was situated off of a long narrow Lane, surrounded by lots of residential homes with, much to the relief of our blokes several public houses were also close by, the publicans in the area must have thought it was V.E day again! The crowd by lunch time was approaching 5 or 6 thousand men, and it was growing, the locals had never seen anything like it. Again it was the press who were keeping us posted as to the goings on in other places, it appeared that the court would issue the tipstaff the warrant for the arrest; he would then be accompanied by police officers to take the three men into custody. The B.B.C radio car informed us that the court intended issuing the warrant at 2 p.m, with the arrest of our members taking place at about 3 p.m, the crowd had now grown to about 8 to 10 thousand trade unionists, and a good few of our blokes were the worst for wear, the beer was beginning to take over. The police

Death of the Docks

sensing that there might be trouble had a meeting with us; we assured them that it was out of our hands, adding that we did not want any violence.

As three o/clock approached the crowd had swelled to something approaching 15,000, the mood was generally very light hearted, and some of the local pubs had run out of beer! The police increased the size of their force but generally we had it under control, we had our own stewards keeping an eye out for the fringe groups who were known as the primary cause of a lot of trouble at rallies or meetings, you instantly knew who they were as it seemed that they had boycotted soap for the last year or so. What took place next must have had some bearing on the final outcome; all of a sudden several hundred dockworkers circled the three and began to chant "you won't take them "I don't know how many men made up the barricade but what I did know was that the tipstaff and the police were not going to get them without a battle royal. The commander of police pleaded with us to let the men be taken into custody peacefully, we informed him truthfully that it was now out of our hands. We never the less pleaded with our men to calm down, but they were having none of it, the situation was growing steadily worse. I saw this as the working class with their backs to the wall, this was the spirit shown in defeating Hitler so what chance did Donaldson have? Then a bombshell was dropped, at about 3o/clock the B.B.C radio van had received an update on the situation, they called me over and informed me that the men were not going to be arrested, something had taken place in Chancery Lane, but the bottom line was they were not being taken into custody.

No-one was sure as to what was going on or what had taken place, one thing that was sure was that we had to get away from here, we informed the men as best as we could as to what was going on and told them to go home. My

Dad was leaving the industry that very day, he had to take his severance pay as my mum was in poor health and he wanted to spend more time looking after her. My parents home was no more than 800 yards from Chobham Farm so I suggested that we head for their home to escape the press and television crews, we quickly made our way there and what we found out still to this day amazes me, the government had a post that was filled by a solicitor, the title for this never used job was "The Official Solicitor", it appeared that the gentleman who held this post was there to represent people who were Insane and unable to represent themselves, the government had got him to attend Chancery Lane to represent the three dockworkers.

It appeared that as this chap had appeared for our three "insane" members that was that! This wanted some believing, however it seemed the government had extracted themselves out of a corner. My Mum and Dad gave our men drinks while they worked on a press statement, the press and television crews had now positioned themselves outside my parent's home waiting to see the three dockers. What an end it was for my Dad after doing more than 25 years in the docks who else could boast to such an end? It was a complete and utter victory for us, the government and the courts had capitulated on a scale not seen before. We could now get back to our original business of getting our work back.

What we did discover after the dust had settled was that some 30,000 dockworkers had come out on strike in support of our three men who had been threatened with jail just for attempting to defend our livelihoods, but if we thought that we had seen Donaldson off then dream on, like any animal that is mortally wounded, this is when they are most dangerous. He was to lash out very viciously and very

Death of the Docks

soon, and it was to be his old chum Lord Vestey who would attempt to rescue the ailing court.

Both barking container base and Chobham Farm were making the right noises about employing registered Dock Workers, so we could be forgiven if we seemed a little bit light headed, with things going our way we now had to plot our next move, however until both container bases employed registered labour the picket line would remain in place, there was a vast difference of opinion amongst the shop stewards committee as to where to move on to next.

The makeup of the committee was much diversified with all age groups covered and all political parties had members who were shop stewards on the committee, the largest single political party whose members were also shop stewards was not surprisingly the communist party. Most of the Shop Stewards belonging to the Communist were aged about 50 years old, they had always served the men in a fashion that could not be questioned, and they had been the voice of the men, always putting the men before any political views or outside influences. The elder element of the shop stewards who held no particular political views would usually support their views on policies, whilst the younger generation of shop stewards let the amount of leg work and ground work do the talking for them, it was in the main the younger element of the shop stewards and their followers who had knocked over Chobham Farm, these had been the backbone of the action, so when they suggested where to go next all hell broke loose.

We wanted to move onto a container base some half a mile from Chobham Farm, it would have given us hundreds of jobs, this is what was needed to employ all the surplus labour, we had done a survey on the place and it would pose no problems to our pickets.

The container base was called London International Freight Terminal, it was however generally known as the

LIFT, and it was one of the largest container bases in the country. This was to be our goal, however the shop stewards committee were divided on whether this should be our next port of call. We were holding meetings in Birmingham to gauge the success that other ports were having, and to consider trying to force the trade unions into taking over our campaign (I don't think so), all in all we were very happy with the way everything was progressing, again we scented victory. It was at a report back meeting to the London port shop stewards on a Friday lunchtime when a member of the unions executive committee came into the hall, he was Brian Nicholson a docker who had worked in Tooley Street docks, he asked if he could make an announcement what followed literally blew us away. He told us that 5 writs had been issued for the immediate arrest of three pickets plus the chairman and secretary of the shop stewards committee.

This time it was Lord Vesteys cold store in Hackney, the midland cold storage depot. The three men named where Derrick Watkins, Connie Clancy and Tony Merrick , these men had been the backbone of picketing this depot, added to the writ again were Vic Turner and Bernie Steers from the shop stewards committee. There was no time to organise anything as the writs had been issued, so the police were out looking for the five men, they were to be taken to Pentonville Prison We returned to our own docks to inform everyone that this time there was to be no official receiver stepping in, that the men were to be picked up and taken to Pentonville Prison, not surprisingly everyone stopped work immediately.

We had been caught unawares and as a result we had not laid any plans, a few of us quickly held a meeting, to decide what was the best way to tackle the struggle we were faced with. We knew that this just had not happened; it had been planned down to the last detail with the prime

Death of the Docks

factor being we were in the peak holiday season, most of the mines, factories and other large Industries were closed for their annual holidays, also it being a Friday afternoon most of the industries that were still actually at work would be winding down for the weekend. It would fall generally to the younger shop stewards to do all the leg work, but without the help and experience of some of the older shop stewards we would not have been able to achieve as much as we did. The first thing that we agreed was to form a picket line outside Pentonville Prison for as long as our men were being held there, furthermore the picket would be a 24 hour picket.   Also two car loads of men would travel to the Continent to ensure that every ship that the ship-owners diverted would be blacked, also to invite them to attend our rallies and demonstrations in our attempt to get our men released. I might add the volunteers who travelled across to the continent were part of the younger members of the shop stewards committee; they had energy levels that ensured you could not lose the dispute.

Then we had to send men to every newspaper in Fleet Street to get them to join the struggle. In short we had to run around at a rate of knots that had never previously been attempted, but circumstances demanded that everyone surpassed there highest expectations. Yet again our dispute had been hijacked by both the conservative party and there anti trade union court being conducted by Donaldson. This time the problem was greater than the last little skirmish we had with them, this time they had our men, and it was up to us to get them out. The police had picked up four of the five men by Friday evening the one that they had not located was Vic Turner, he was out having a drink when the police had called to pick him up, the press and the television made capital of this, they claimed that Vic Turner had gone on the run to avoid being captured by the police. What a load of rubbish.

PENTONVILLE 1972

The next five days of my life could fill a book on its own, not to mention the experiences that I and many others, who put their life on hold so that the jailed London dockers could be released on our terms. But paramount above all personal feelings and exhaustion that was about to take over our lives, was securing the unconditional release of our members. The only way anyone could describe the journey would be a momentous moment in the modern day working class victories.

Yes there have been larger and longer strikes, but this was in my opinion the mother of them all when it comes down to what was achieved against all the odds. We met up outside Pentonville Prison at about 7o/clock on the Friday evening, there were no more than a few dozen pickets at first, we knew that our first port of call was Fleet Street; we had to get the newspapers out on strike, if only to stop them peddling there filth and lies about us. We set off to meet their equivalent of our shop steward system, in Fleet Street they were not called shop stewards but were known as father of the chapels, we visited all the major newspapers to try and get them to join our struggle, each different group of workers had their own father of the chapel, there was the electricians'(E.T.U), you had the print workers(S.O.G.A.T) and the rest of the workers belonged to(N.A.T.S.OP.A) ,each

Death of the Docks

of these groups had their own father of the chapel ,not to mention the journalist who belonged to the N.U.J. Because of our relationship with these we never bothered ourselves with them.

Given that it was the print unions who had led the demonstrations against the anti trade union laws being introduced, and given the fact that they threw everything they could into the marches and demonstrations with huge marching bands leading the proceedings, and when it come to the speakers they again led from the front, so you could be forgiven in thinking that we expected a very favourable reception from their representatives.

The communist party had arranged for us to be met and taken to meet their delegates, without their assistance we would still be trying to get an audience today, it was when we were being taken to meet the father of the chapels at the Sun. The chaps who "escorted" us to meet them informed us of the power that these men had, we took this with a pinch of salt we duly met with them to inform them that our members where in the clink as a direct result of the legislation that they and us had demonstrated against. What happened next threw us of guard, the S.O.G.A.T. chap produced a letter and waving it under our noses proudly announced" we have told the editor that unless this letter condemning the imprisonment of the London dockers is published we will not be printing the papers tonight". Bearing in mind that this group of father of the chapels represented the workers of the Sun newspaper, whose owner Rupert Murdoch (the Australian who became an Englishman only to discover that he wanted to be an American),he was hardly sympathetic to the cause of the registered dockworkers.

We told this father of the chapel that the time for niceties was over, and that nothing short of him asking his members to join the strike would do. He again made reference to this stupid note, we told him that the owner of the Sun would print ten letters if it meant the difference between printing and not printing, it was then that the electricians' father of the chapel interjected by telling us that his members would not be throwing the switches, meaning there would be no newspapers printed at the Sun that night, also that all members would be holding a mass meeting the following day. (I wonder if the same man wanted Murdoch to print a letter condemning the Suns move to Wapping).

As we travelled round the various papers one thing was for sure, the father of the chapels operated on a scale that we had never witnessed, they had minders to watch out for them, some even had secretaries dealing with their correspondence! Slightly different to how we operated. The meeting that was to be held the next day was in fact a gathering of all the father of the chapels, I was down to address them, something to ponder on. But all in all we had met with a good response with the exception of the daily express, A lot of their workers seemed to share their owners views, and word had it that the threats of violence from their own members who had threatened them, led to the daily express being printed with minders everywhere, also the newspaper insisted that a heavy police presence be in attendance every night when the presses were rolling. What a lovely way to earn your living!

Back to Pentonville the picket line had grown, we had left at about 10 p.m to go to Fleet Street, and it was now about 3 a.m, amazingly the number of pickets had increased to 300, and you began to sense a flavour of the atmosphere that was to prevail for the duration of our stay. More groups were arriving as the night wore on, the police asked to meet us, the commander of the police told us that there would have to be a police presence to match the numbers,

Death of the Docks

however he asked us for details of how we intended in "policing" the crowd ourselves, we told him that we would be appointing stewards to watch the crowd and to ensure that no groups of cranks caused trouble, on hearing this he assured us that although he had to engage a large police presence they would in the main remain in the background, this he hoped would not inflame the situation.

As morning arrived we were taken aback with the ever growing crowds, as a new group arrived we tried to find out who they represented and welcoming them, we had not expected a demonstration of this magnitude, we had trade councils, labour party groups and numerous trade union delegations with shop stewards from all over the region ,then the fringe groups that you always got whenever there was a demonstration, the revolutionaries' smelt big trouble and they were appearing on the hour every hour, a group of squatters ,the usual sprinkling of anarchists in fact the most broad minded person would raise the eyebrows in shock at some of them. Taking into account that most dockworkers were not politically correct then some of these groups would not get it all their own way, and they would have learnt a whole new meaning to life. Whilst we needed support from almost anywhere, we could not be distracted from our goal that was the release of our men and with no distractions. Newham labour party had offered us the use of their constituency offices in Plaistow, East London, which we gratefully accepted, B.T engineers rigged us up 2 telephones within an hour, and this must be a world record! But it showed to us that people wanted to do whatever they could to help out. The establishment must have been very confident that they had done us by choosing the end of July to make their move; nearly all of the country's major industries were closed down for the annual holidays, so we had very limited contact facilities available to us.

The television, Radio and those few newspapers that had managed to get scabs to print them, were going into overdrive that Vic Turner, our chairman, had gone on the run to avoid being picked up by the police. He was in fact on the picket line outside Pentonville! I suppose the last place they would look for him was outside the Prison that he was to be locked up in! At about 10 o'clock that morning the press noticed him and he was duly taken into custody.

The main entrance at Pentonville has 2 public houses within a stone's throw of each other, and for the 2 landlords of these 2 public houses their numbers had just come up on the lottery! Without warning these 2 pubs were to be packed out for every minute that they were open, one of them however was the most miserable type of human being you would want to meet, for after taking an absolute fortune every day he then expected the crowd outside to remain silent so that he could get to sleep! Money and misery, this man made Victor Meldrew appear to be happy. But I suppose it takes all kinds.

Events were now moving at a very fast pace, people had managed to make contact with us either directly on the picket line or at the strike headquarters, we had left two people to man the headquarters but it was evident that they required more men there, we were constantly being approached by people who wanted to show their support, or they might request that we send a speaker to address the labour force were they worked, so we had members travelling all over the place to address groups explaining our case. However I did not think that we had to do much explaining to do given the circumstances, probably the best of all the people who wanted to speak to us were the journalist, they approached us, displaying their N.U.J card and heaping sympathy on our cause, not coming up for air they would continue by attacking the government for imprisoning trade unionists, they were good, in fact some

Death of the Docks

of them could have picked up an Oscar for the "best actor" category. We gave them travelling instructions in dockology terms. This is for those of you not familiar with such terms you tell someone to F... Off.

They knew no depths that they would sink to, they were, as one leading trade union leader described them as prostituting themselves for a story, to liken them with prostitutes is doing the ladies of the night a disservice, as at least they offer their clients a chance of a few moments of happiness, the journalist offer you nothing and in many cases they can ruin your life. But they always defend themselves by agreeing with you, you then read their story and it is completely different. When you challenge them they claim that it was there editor who changed their story. So it came as no great surprise when we decided to have nothing to do with them. We also had certain trade union leaders telling us that we had dug a large hole for ourselves and we were now buried in it, these were senior trade union officials and they were given the same travelling instructions as the journalists had received. Who needed enemies when you had friends like these people .I've no doubt that the few trade union leaders making these sounds were the ones who had defied the T.U.C ruling in having nothing to do with the national industrial relations court.

What our critics did not like was to be reminded of the struggles and sacrifices that the working class movement had made over the years; we had no time for the so called representatives of the working classes, making their fancy speeches more often than not trying to justify what they had done. The hard truth was that they had sold out, and by attacking us they were trying to ease their consciences (if they had one).Those who had the bottle to attend the picket line usually left with a flea in their ear, what they reported back to their committees heaven only knows. What they had done by registering with the court had set the trade union movement back light years.

Our priority that Saturday was to attend the meeting in the city of the fathers of the chapels for the whole of Fleet Street, we had to cut off the filth that the likes of Murdoch and his cronies would peddle. Once we had the print workers on our side we could get on with getting our men released without the unwarranted propaganda being used against our every move.It was just before I was due to speak to the print workers that someone drew to my attention about a statement that Reg Prentice M.P. had made.   Prentice was an M.P. for the area in which I lived, therefore he represented many dockworkers and their families, he had said "that the dockers had set out to be martyrs, and now that they had achieved that status by getting themselves jailed, the authorities should throw away the keys "The same view that is held today by an overwhelming number of the population hold today, about the representatives in Parliament(M.Ps & Lords) over the thieving of tax payers money under the guise of expenses. Prentice had never been flavour of the month with many of the trade unions, but this really took the biscuit. It seemed that the man had a death wish, a wish that was later granted to him when he was de-selected, this being a posh word for thrown out, he later found his true roots by joining the conservative party before losing his seat and fading away, faster than the docks he once represented

.

Never the less the meeting of the fathers of the chapels took place and I put our case very briefly, as I did not think that there was much to explain, the decision that they took left everything to the imagination, you could view it from four different sides and come up with four different views, but most of the print workers joined the strike leaving most of the country without their Sunday or any daily

Death of the Docks

newspapers. Again the exception to the rule was the Daily and Sunday Express who printed, the father of the chapel told us that although his members were working they would not print any extra copies, this he added would stop express newspapers from gaining extra circulation because of the other papers being on strike, how very benevolent of them! As one striking print worker told us "they must read and believe the filth that their employers print"! To make them feel comfortable while all their colleagues were out on strike they had to work with armed guards and heavies protecting them. What depths would some people stoop to?

With the messages coming in offering support as soon as the mines and factories re-opened we began to feel slightly optimistic that we could win this dispute. I seed to have drawn the short straw, for like many others I was to help run the strike headquarters by day and when I was finished there I had to take charge of the pickets outside Pentonville prison by night. By my reckoning this left me with no hours to spend at home with my family, and as we had only just moved into the place , most of the packing cases hadn't even been emptied, my wife was not best pleased with me. Saturday evening and the crowd was still growing, it now stretched for some800 yards and was 8 -10 deep in places, what we had done was to keep our blokes on the side of the road that was directly outside the prison, we had put all the strange groups of people on the opposite side, this way we knew generally where everyone was.

One of our blokes told me that there was someone who wanted to see me, he then took me across the road and introduced me to these two men who could have been impersonating Ronnie and Reggie Kray, I shook hands with them and discovered that they were Irish, they "escorted" me down the side street into an alleyway, I actually thought that I was to meet my maker, to make matters worse I was alone. All of a sudden this woman appears from now where, she holds out her hand to shake mine, with relief I responded "Hello" she boomed," a great turn out." She was in a combat coat and trousers, I thought we had another crank, and then she delivered a broadside."You have got enough men here and we can supply the guns and hand grenades to get your men out of there". There didn't appear to be a lot that I could say, I thanked her very much for her kind offer but told her that we would have to decline her offer as we intended on getting our men out in a peaceful way, she looked at me as if I were mad and left. I returned back to the safety of our own crowd, relieved that I had lived to tell the tale.

Some months later a lady in Northern Ireland stole some of her parent's art collection and acquired a helicopter with some of the proceeds and flew over the Maze Prison and helped some fellow I.R.A. member's escape. The lady in question? Dr Rose Dugdale. Boring old life isn't it?

Most of our men were killing an hour or two by having a beer or two, and as many of the other demonstrators had never encountered the likes of our blokes, it was indeed a sight to behold, tales that Uncle Albert would have been proud of where being told to eager listeners', the listening crowd couldn't get enough of it, they gladly bought beers for them and settled back for more adventures. Another little group who introduced themselves as some solidarity group, they told us that they had a house nearby and that we were welcome to use it for a snack or a wash and brush up, although I must add at this point that the chap making the offer seemed as though he had been boycotting soap for a fair good while, however we thought that this was a great offer and agreed not to tell too many people in case it spoiled the house. We went round there only to find that they were a group of squatters and had been occupying this house for some time, the place was an absolute tip, hygiene

Death of the Docks

was never their main concern, and they always seemed to have a saucepan of stew on the go. Although I could never bring myself to taste it; however I must say that the squatters were first class people.

Saturday night outside the prison was an experience to saviour; the local pubs had practically been drunk dry, after throwing out time we settled down for the night, the usual assortment of chauffer driven cars would stop and peer at us, some of the revellers returning home from dinner in the West End of London, would make the fatal mistake of leaving there cars to tell us that they had discussed our dispute over dinner, adding that they thought what we were doing was a wonderful thing! They were told were to go in the best dockland terminology. However at about 1 a.m the crowd decided to have a sing-song, what followed was the most moving moment of the entire campaign outside the prison. A few of our pickets were having a sing song, when all of a sudden everyone burst into song, when everyone joined in singing you'll Never Walk Alone the whole place resembled Liverpool football ground.

The whole moment was capped off when the prisoners started waving blankets and sheets from their cell windows, after they had been released our members said that moment gave them the biggest lift that they could have had, considering that the prison was set well back from where we were picketing the singing must have carried a mighty long way, one person who never appreciated it was the publican from the nearby pub, he threw open the window and screamed "some of us are trying to get some sleep!", the replies that were hurled in his direction are unprintable. Then our members and the whole gathering started singing the red flag, this brought about more sheets and blankets being waved from the cell windows, our men inside the jail told us when they had been released that this had been the defining moment for them, "we knew you all meant business out there when we heard that"

We held a meeting to evaluate the situation on Sunday morning, as more dockers and shop stewards where arriving from ports all over the country our meetings had more of a national feel about them, one of the first things that we agreed was to call for a mass march on the prison, it was agreed so as to give ourselves the chance of organising that the march and demonstration would take place on Tuesday, which was by a coincidence the same day that the general counsel of the T.U.C were meeting to discuss the crisis. By another strange twist of fate on that very same day Parliament were voting on the crisis, some M.Ps belonging to the labour party (NOT Reg Prentice!) had put down a motion condemning the government for setting up the court in Chancery Lane, and for the government to release the 5 London dockworkers immediately with a pardon and the apologies of the House.

Such wonders, we appeared to be gaining friends! But hold on, the government intended to impose a three line whip to ensure that they carried the day. The television and the radio were giving the dispute blanket coverage, and they badly wanted interviews from the shop stewards movement, we had unfortunately for them, passed a resolution stating that the only media interviews to be given would have to be live, no more interviews where the editor edits out what he wants and leaves the whole interview to be shown totally different to what had been said. So that put paid to that side of the exercise, the media would not consider allowing us to be interviewed live for the fear of the public finding out the truth. We had to split ourselves into groups to cover everything that was going on, I was to attend the meeting being held by the T.U.C in Great Russell Street, then on to Parliament with a group of shop stewards from the national port shop stewards committee, also I was

Death of the Docks

to do a live radio interview on B.B.C Radio London with Jimmy Carpenter, he was chairman of the shop stewards committee for the Port of London Authority. It was the breakfast show and after being interviewed there was to be a phone in, this could be interesting. Despite the fact that it was Sunday delegations were arriving constantly, some to join the picket, while others just to spend a day with the protesters and to find out what was being planned.

We sensed by the amount of people that were arriving that something that this country had never witnessed was about to unfold, even the big players in the trade unions were sending their big guns done to see us; you had to be seen around the Pentonville Prison area! What we also sensed was that many of the big unions and plenty of the smaller ones saw this situation as a way of smashing Donaldson, his kangaroo court, and the Tory government into submission. We were about to be used by all and sundry to do the dirty work that they never had the bottle to do. But it was a catch 22 situation, we needed every bit of help that we could get, while the big players hid behind our actions, not daring to show there open support for the fear of recriminations from Donaldson.

So we had to make do with the old fashioned "nod and a wink" method, but we knew that through their massive networks of communications that, again, if we wanted their "unofficial" help then we had to accept the position as it was. A dispute brings out the best in people, or so goes the saying, one union leader who never allowed the best to be brought out was the electricians' leader; this man was a right winger who thought that anyone who questioned his beliefs was a communist. Never mind as to whether the cause was a just one, he would just condemn out of hand any action that was being taken as a communist conspiracy, he was the standard bearer for the right wing, and when he declared of our members in prison that" they were getting what they deserve "it come as no surprise to either us or any other Trade Unionist. This man must have checked under his bed every night to see if there were any commos under it. As most of our members never belonged to the do gooders brigade, the "outsiders" who had joined the picket line had never encountered anything or anyone who could tell a tale how they could, so all the way along the picket lines you saw groups of people being entertained by our blokes, it was a better show than the royal command performance! But as I walked along the lines of people at about 3 a.m on a Sunday morning I was at a loss to find anything that could be considered on the same scale, no this was a moment to cherish, and without a doubt working class history was in the making.

What this proved was that despite the obstacles and despite all the might of the system being against you, if you stick together then nothing is beyond your reach. This was a once in a lifetime experience, many of you would have missed what was occurring as the newspapers were not being printed. So next time you feel that a huge injustice is being imposed on you, don't adopt the British approach and shrug your shoulders and sigh what can you do? Get out there and make one, while everybody thinks that nothing can be done, nothing will be done. And that's just the way they want it.

Sunday and the police ask to meet with us to explain that they are getting concerned at the size of the demonstrators outside the prison, we inform them that we are keeping an eye on the situation with a view to turn away potential trouble makers, the police estimated that the crowd this morning was in the region of 6,000 people. The police accept our assurances with the proviso of using their own men to control the crowds if needs have it. What we never told the police (although I'm sure they knew) was that the crowds next week could exceed figures not dreamed of, and

Death of the Docks

we also forgot to inform them of the offer we had from the Irish contingent.

Feeling left out of it and being the person responsible for the state the country was in, Lord Vestey decided to put in his twopenneth. He again reiterated that dockworkers were welcome to work at his cold storage depots as long as they had taken their severance pay from the dock Industry. He was beginning to sound like a long playing record. No mention was made that not only was he the cause of this trouble, but it was he who was instrumental in getting the ship-owners to take us on, be it in the docks or as was the more likely outside in container depots or cold stores. Not once did Lord Vestey ever attempt to defend the position of not employing registered dock labour in the depots outside the docks. What Vestey did tell the media was he understood our concerns and as such made his offer to the unions. He knew this was not acceptable and it was a red rag to a bull. However the public read into the good Lords statement as dockers receiving a redundancy cheque one day and the good Lord giving you a job the next day. No-one had worked out that his derisory offer was not at all feasible, thousands of dockworkers had lost their jobs and his cold storage plant in Hackney could at best give us 25 jobs. The media seemed to have overlooked this point.

Sunday night saw the usual stream of inquisitive visitors who "just happened to be passing" so we thought we would stop and wish you luck, we needed their good wishes like you needed a hole in the head. Probably the strangest visitor we had every night was when a black taxi would stop and leave a case of Guinness, he made absolutely no comment as to where he had "picked up his fare." Knowing near enough what time the taxi would arrive with our benefactors' gift, we were ready for him tonight and when he arrived we asked him who was sending us the Guinness, all we ever found out that the fare had been collected from a senior labour politician, we later learned without concrete evidence that our "nightcap" was being sent by a labour politician who would be prime minister again quite soon. Cheers Harold.

We had a rare opportunity on Sunday night to reflect on what had gone on and how we saw the next few days, although with the speed that events were happening, I think that Nostradamus would have struggled to predict as to what would unfold. What we did know was that our own dispute had been blown right of course, and we would have to tread very carefully to get our campaign back on track, nothing was ever going to eclipse this dispute.Taking everything into account we had to be pleased with the support we were getting from all quarters, the next couple of days would be crucial to us getting our men out of prison, but the moral of our men inside was good and given that the rest of the prisoners inside were "treating our men" favourably. The set up was that the prison governor would ask our men each morning if they were sorry for showing contempt to the court, not once did any of our men waver. They were receiving plenty of visitors who were keeping them informed as to what was happening outside.

Monday morning and we were off to the B.B.C radio studios to do the live breakfast show and phone in, it was all going fairly well in fact the radio show had listeners phoning in saying what nice people we were! The leader of the lorry drivers phoned up to question our rights to work in container bases, we put him right and what took place next could only be described as unbelievable, the presenter of the show thanked us for attending and asked if there was anything we would like to add before the show finished. Jimmy Carpenter then launched into a plea on the rights of

Death of the Docks

dockworkers to work in container bases, and as a result of our members pursuing their rights in attempting to correct this injustice 5 of our men were in the slammer. He then made an impassioned plea for all trade unionists listening to stop work and join the strike to get them released. This must be the only time that the B.B.C has carried a broadcast calling for an all out strike!

That day saw more activity from the powers to be than you could ever possibly imagine, the T.G.W.U. announced that it was calling a re-called dock delegate conference on that Thursday to discuss one subject only. That was to be dock work. This would include our call on container bases to be examined and the threat of non-scheme ports. Normally the announcement of the unions intentions of dealing with our problem would be received with open arms however we viewed this very suspiciously indeed, why all of a sudden had the trade union taken an active interest in our dispute?.

We viewed their move as one to undermine the men in prison. They were being visited each day by a member of the executive committee of our union, so they could ferry in the news that the trade union were about to take over the dispute, so why prolong the stay in prison. This was typical of what the unions represented, they always speak with double meanings, what they were really saying to our members in jail was end this today, as we are going to take up the fight to regain our work. We dismissed the Trade Unions move as one of no consequence. But whether we liked it or not the trade union seemed to be appearing on the scene, at the time we had not noticed that they were about to wrest control of the dock industry from us. We all agreed that as much as we would like to discuss the problem with the T.G.W.U, our priority was the release of our men. This was a bitter pill them to swallow. They wanted to meet with us to discuss what we wanted! Not that we had told them for the last several years. We had to focus our attention on one thing without any distractions and that was the release of our members. The news coming in was all good news more groups of workers who had returned to work on Monday morning had decided to come out on strike in support of us, and it was growing bigger by the hour.

Then we received the visitor we had all hoped and waited for, the delegate from the National Union of Mineworkers gave us an assurance that on returning from their annual holidays they would join the struggle. Although the T.U.C had met we could not find out what if anything they had agreed, all we were told was that the general counsel of the T.U.C were meeting first thing on Tuesday morning. No-one from the T.U.C bothered getting in touch with us. So taking their track record in supporting the working class, we assumed that for any of the important big wigs to be seen talking with us was beneath them. They saw our dispute and the 5 dockworkers in prison as a tool that could smash the anti trade union laws.

The picket outside the prison had now grown to alarming proportions, so much so that the police told us that they could not stand by and see it increase any more, they bumbled on about safety and the rights of people who live locally, but they were unable to tell us what they proposed as an alternative or what they would do to keep the numbers down. Back at our strike H.Q the shop stewards who were running it reported to us that they had been receiving some very strange phone calls and visitors, people who would not associate themselves with unofficial committees, our H.Q

Death of the Docks

reported that the "vibes" that they had picked up indicated that something big was about to happen.

We told our reps at the strike H.Q if they continued to get visitors bearing cryptic messages then they should advise the visitors to attend the prison where the national port shop stewards committee had a huge contingent in attendance, but I think this was beneath many of them, not just to be seen there but to be talking to us!Can you begin to imagine what was taking place behind the scenes? the T.U.C. were meeting, the cabinet was in session and to top it all Jack Jones was on the phone to anybody who he thought might be able to bring about an end to this dispute. I might add at this point that the blue union who had 3 of the5 imprisoned dockworkers, never attempted to put their 3 members under any pressure to conform on the contrary they declared the strike official! Vic Feather who was general secretary of the T.U.C had seen many of the trade unions register to avoid stringent financial penalties, these unions would later have to pay the penalty with the T.U.C, but the immediate problem that the T.U.C was faced with was that 5 London Dockers were in prison for supporting the trade unions policy of not recognising the national industrial relations court.

What you are about to read is an accurate account of what actually happened, you will find no references anywhere, it was as if it had not happened. In checking out details of dates and times of events I was unable to locate any of the details on any web site. It was as if it never took place, I know that many of the newspapers were on strike so their archives would not contain details, but the B.B.C and I.T.N news archives contain nothing about the imprisonment of our members. What still amazes me to this very day is the fact that the general counsel of the T.U.C voted to call for a 24hour general strike, they informed the government that unless the 5 London Dockers were released then a 24 hour general strike would take place.

Now, how often have you known the T.U.C to adopt a militant role? In fact can you ever re-call them adopting such a stance? Not since 1926 when they took over the miners' strike, by calling a general strike and then selling them out, has the T.U.C ever done anything that remotely resembled there being in touch with the membership that they purport to represent. That was the first major development that carried hardly any coverage in the media; can you imagine such important news being ignored today? In defence of the media the T.U.C seemed so embarrassed by the decision that they kept it quiet, however I am sure the media hacks were fully aware of what was going on.

Then you had the mass demonstration on Tuesday, if the capital has seen or indeed had seen a march that was a large as this then I must have missed it, this was without doubt the largest gathering that anyone could remember, and there were seasoned protesters making this observation. The march went through the city and onwards to Pentonville , so large was the march that when the head of the march began to arrive at the prison there were still people waiting to set out back at the start! City workers had hurled abuse at the marchers as it snaked its way through the city, they would throw things towards the marchers from their offices that were situated 2 or 3 floors high, showing what cowards they were.

Every trade unionist worth his salt appeared to be in the march, some had even left there holidays early to demonstrate, taking everything into account that the dispute was only a few days old this sent out warning signs to the government that this was not going to be tolerated. Young girls and office managers who hurled abuse from the safe sanctuary of their offices probably were avid sun readers and believed every word that they printed, I only hope that as they have grown older and wiser that they have learnt that with the sun newspaper, you always check the newspapers' date as in all probability the will be the only piece of truth contained in the entire newspaper.

Another shameful episode that marred the march was the behaviour of our own members towards Bernadette Devlin, she was a new M.P representing the catholic minority in Belfast, she had been seen by the media making explosive arms to use against the British troops in Belfast. She got the same media coverage that the dockworkers received; this was because she would not conform to the rules made by the gentlemen's club at the House of Corruption. Our blokes spit on her, pushed and jostled her and hurled abuse towards her. Yet she still marched all the way with our blokes, she had walked every yard of the demonstration to show solidarity with us, unlike many of the celebrities who like to be photographed as one of the marchers when in fact they probably joined the march for the last 800 yards, these people are known as Hollywood demonstrators, they are only there when the photographers were on the scene. Later that day I would meet up with Bernadette Devlin in the House of Commons. I tried to apologise for what had taken place but she would have none of it, "Don't worry about it" she said-and she meant it, I suppose the area she represented had seen far greater scenes than our march that day.

The national port shop stewards committee had been invited to meet up with a group of Labour M.Ps, they were mainly left wing M.Ps and they invited us to the bar in the House of Corruption, this was an education in its own right, the only people allowed in the bar are of course M.Ps and their guests, no one but an M.P is allowed to buy drinks from the bar (I suppose this stops you working out how heavily the bar is being subsidised). The group of M.Ps consisted of some M.Ps whose constituencies took in areas with a large percentage of the constituency being made up by voters who depend on the docks as their livelihoods. Before you think that we had gone there just to get on the lash, let me tell you that the sum total of our alcoholic consumption was 1 pint of beer, this was offered to us in 2 rounds of drinks where you received a half a pint each shout! I could have remained behind and had a drink with the M.P, who seemed taken with me and the work that I was putting in to get our men released, all he kept on about was what a tremendous job we were doing and he singled me out for exceptional praise. Little did I know that it was my backside that he was after! I received a tap on the shoulder from a very well known M.P who advised me that this particular M.P was a homosexual, adding that he preferred boys rather than girls! The speed that I moved away from him made Linford Christy look slow.

Barbara Castle was sitting up by the bar and looking the worst for wear, I was now sitting with another M.P, I asked him if she was all right, the whole group of M.Ps told us that she was to remain away from the floor of the house during the debate on the imprisoned dockworkers, as the tories would have a field day at her expense because she had previously tried to introduce in place of strife, another piece of Parliamentary legislation that was anti trade union. But as there was a three line whip all M.Ps, drunk or sober would be required to vote. Harold Wilson the leader of the labour party had reserved us a group of seats in the strangers gallery to hear the debate, as we went to take our seats the whole house broke out into a buzz, and then everybody stared up in our direction, they had heard that we were the national port shop stewards, we were the people responsible for the plight of the country. If seven or eight Martians had taken their seats I don't think they would have

Death of the Docks

been given such a strange look.It was then that Bernadette Devlin asked to see us, two of us quickly left our seats to meet her, we again apologised to her for the treatment that our blokes had dished out towards her, she wouldn't hear of an apology, stating it was an honour for her to march alongside British dockworkers, the difference between her and the other M.Ps we had met was that she meant it. I told her that I did not agree with the I, R.A.s tactics, in fact I informed her that 99.9% of the population condemned what they were doing, but I have to say that whether or not you agreed with her beliefs I still believe that she was the only M.P who never sold her soul in order to remain in Parliament. She never accepted the"trappings"that suck you in to be part of the system.

As the debate got under way both sides of the house try to score points against each other, it was when the Prime Minister (Ted Heath) made reference to us as bully boys turning up at an innocent businessman's premises and begin to picket it, leading to the man either caving in to our demands or to resist and face the likelihood of going out of business. I have never heard such a load of crap, I sent down a message to the labour front bench that "the small innocent man whose business was being picketed was no less a person than Lord Vestey. The labour front bench chose to ignore this until it had been checked out by their researchers, by which time it would be too late. We decided to leave at this point knowing that there was some 600+ M.Ps playing at the game. Well we were not playing and unless they released our men the struggle would only intensify.

Just as we were about to leave the chamber the sergeant at arms approached me waving this piece of paper, it was a message from the B.B.Cs political correspondent asking to meet with him by the St. Stephens entrance. We went along to be met by Ian Ross (no relation) who informed us that the B.B.C were putting on a special Panorama that evening, covering the ever growing crisis because of the imprisoned dockers. What he wanted to do was to record an interview with one or two of us, and broadcast it during the programme that evening, when he was informed that we only did "live" broadcasts, he assured us that any such recording would not be taken out of context, when asked who else was to appear he rattled of some M.Ps names and a representative of the container bases that we were picketing. Strangely enough they all would be appearing on the programme live as it went out, when we politely declined the offer Ian Ross tried to assure us that the only reason that we hadn't been asked to appear, was that due to the fact that the studio where they normally film Panorama, was unavailable and that the studio they had was not big enough to hold everyone. Now I put it to you, do you not think that this was not challenging our intelligence? We declined the invitation and wished him every success with the show.

Now I would point out at this stage that we knew nothing about the decision that the T.U.C had taken, to call a 24 hour general strike, but be under no illusions whatsoever the government and the leader of the opposition knew as did the B.B.C. But not a word had been uttered to give us or anybody else a clue as to what was going on. In a final roll of the dice Ian Ross agreed to our request by allowing a representative to appear live on the show, we had had enough, so in order to get away from his persistent pestering we told him that unless the whole of the committee appeared then no one would appear. That done the job and we returned to the real world.

The size of the demonstration outside Pentonville was now at an all time high, you had to fight your way through

Death of the Docks

the crowd. It was so thick that it was reaching worryingly proportions, many people who had been on the march had decided to stay and continue the protest by remaining outside the prison. The sight outside the prison was indeed one to behold, the groups who had attended the march had brought their trade union banners with them and they adorned the whole area, it was indeed a sight that I knew that I probably would never see again.

By now I was getting tired, sleep had become a luxury, at best you would sit on the pavement in the early hours of the morning and try and get a couple of hours sleep, but tonight I was feeling very tired, one of the shop stewards told me to go around to the squatters house and get a proper sleep, the thought of this seemed to give me a fresh lease of life! I was not and I am still not a snob, but the thought of getting your head down in the squat made me cringe, you envisaged that you would be admitted the hospital for tropical diseases', but many of our pickets spent a few hours round there and nothing happened to them! Again the welcome they gave us made up for any of the luxuries that they never had, but I still wouldn't sleep there.

Wednesday morning broke and I made my way back to the strike H.Q at Plaistow, this took a good 45 minutes to make the transfer and I normally arrived back at about 8.a m, usually we would exchange any relevant details that might have taken place, this morning was an exceptional day, bearing in mind of the events that had taken place over the last 24 hours. The shop steward who was organising everything at the strike H.Q was Bill Chapman, he was later to become Mayor of Newham, it was he who logged all the phone calls or recorded personal callers, and lo and behold it was he who answered the telephone and called for quiet and for us all to stop talking, we knew something was up by the look on his face, when he had finished the call he excitedly informed us that the caller was from the docker who was an Executive member for the T.G.W.U, he had informed us that the 5 men were to be released at 10 a. m that morning. Victory was ours.

I felt so knackered that instead of returning to Pentonville to witness the victorious scenes of the mother of all victories with the release of our men I went home for the first time since last Friday, the kids must have wondered who I was! But I needed some sleep, so I took to my bed for a few hours sleep.

It emerged later on in the morning that the government had exhumed the corpse of the official solicitor to appear in the kangaroo court in Chancery Lane. Later on that afternoon I received a phone call saying that all our little group of shop stewards would be going out tonight to celebrate, many of the other national port shop stewards were coming along. It was on with your glad rags and out to celebrate, we had a grand night and to round of the festivities I invited everyone back to my home to continue the celebrations!

Now, my wife was not best pleased , as we had not long moved into this home, and the fact that we had 3 young children, the youngest being just 3 months old , coupled together with that we had not even finished unpacking, much of our stuff was still in tea chests, and the lights were just a naked light bulb with no lampshades, I tried to reassure her that these people" were your own kind", and they were not coming to our home to hold an inspection, I suppose after visiting the squat anywhere was luxury, the fact that we hadn't even unpacked coupled with that it was a Wednesday night and as we had just moved in what would our new neighbours think of us, I was not in the mood for reasoning and everyone(about 30 people) came round home to continue the celebrations.

A grand time was had by all, and as the T.G.WU were holding the re-called docks delegate conference at 11 a.m

Death of the Docks

the next day when we finished drinking most of the shop stewards who were also delegates at the conference from Liverpool, Hull, Southampton and Preston just stayed and dossed down for a few hours, I was in for a shock when I got up in the morning ,one of our shop stewards who was a real character had got everyone up and cleared up the mess that had been made from the empties and the overflowing ashtrays, in fact he had even mopped the floor!

He then phoned a mini-cab firm and ordered several min-cabs, and took the shop stewards who had stayed at my place overnight out for breakfast. Not to the local cafe oh no, you're now dealing with Tony and Tony does not do half measures! He had the cabbie take them to one of London's plushest hotels The Dorchester. Being greeted on arrival by the head waiter Tony declared that "they were all here for breakfast, and would begin with bucks fizz", he also informed the head waiter that everyone would require a fresh buttonhole, the Liverpool shop stewards could hardly believe what was happening, after having the waiters recommendation, poached haddock washed down with more fine champagne the bill was sent for, the waiter duly presented Tony with the bill who then requested to see the head waiter." Is there a problem Sir?" enquired the head waiter, "I trust everything was to Sirs satisfaction". Most certainly replied Tony in fact it exceeded our expectations, however we don't have any money then launching into a general description of that they were shop stewards from every major port in the country and that the breakfast that they had just had was to good just to be enjoyed by the ruling class. The head waiter never even flinched "would sir and his company just leave quietly?"So with everyone well fed and watered it was onwards to Transport House. Name me another person who would even think about doing that, not to mention actually having the front to do it!

THE AFTERMATH

We expected nothing from the trade union; the meeting had been called at the insistence of the unions general secretary, Jack Jones. It was to attempt to resolve the growing problem of both the un-attached register and the non scheme ports. Bearing in mind that every trade union in the country was living in fear of Black John Donaldson and his court, no-one expected too much from this conference, however what had not been taken into account when the meeting had been arranged was the state of euphoria that everyone was in. The mood was one that I had never witnessed before, with delegates who could not be described as militants in the mood for a fight, after what had just taken place everyone thought that we were the" bees knees", and that we could conquer Everest, run a Marathon and then swim the Channel!

This was our moment and no-one was going to take it away from us.

But even the most optimistic of us could not envisage the trade union calling an official strike. Whilst all the delegates were inside debating what to do we retired for a cup of tea and a sandwich, amid much back slapping and congratulating each other, on what was a truly remarkable achievement given the mountain that we had faced and conquered it. The revolutionary parties were still tagging on to us; I suppose given what had taken place they must

Death of the Docks

have sensed a revolution! But they were still aggravating us by telling us where we were going wrong! They have always had that air of superiority about them, they certainly fit into the" we know what's best for you brigade."The meeting inside Transport House never lasted very long, and word had escaped from the conference hall to us outside that they had voted for a official strike to commence immediately, the question of dock work was now firmly on the unions agenda. The strange thing about it was that the non-scheme ports had abstained from the vote, so too did a lot smaller ports, in fact when you examine the vote you should have known it would end in tears. The voting went38-28 to strike, with18 abstaining from the vote, so the 18 delegates who "kindly" abstained because they never had the problem to the extent that the major ports had, held the key, it would be the18 abstentions' that would ultimately hold the key for the future of our Industry.

But right now that was the least of our worries, the T&G.W.U had at last seized the problem with both hands and we believed that they would sort it out, however before a word had been spoken about ways of resolving the dispute the executive committee of the T&G.W.U issued a strangely worded statement, basically it read that whilst appreciating the problem within the dock industry they had an obligation to all the workers currently employed in the container bases.(Especially the ones that held a T.&G.W.U card.) Again we chose to ignore this because we to never wanted fellow workers sacked, but the executive knew this so why issue such a statement?

Despite failing to spot the warning lights we were jubilant, our general secretary, Jack Jones held a press conference where he surpassed himself in explaining to the media why the trade union wanted the problem solved, once and for all. But another warning light that had been missed was from a piece of advice my Dad had given to me, he claimed that the trade union (the T&G.W.U) only ever became involved or took over an unofficial dispute when it was so successful that the only way to end it was to take over the dispute, having taken over the dispute they, and not the unofficial leaders or the men, would bring about an end to the dispute. All rather clever isn't it?

The government set up an enquiry into the troubles in Britain's docks, the enquiry this time would consist of a committee who knew of the problems that had led to the current situation, and that it would have joint chairmen, Jack Jones our general secretary and Lord Aldington, the current chairman of the Port of London Authority, and they had to produce a report to the government in a short space of time. Well that was the official position, the shop stewards committee met again amongst jubilant scenes; we had held meetings of the men to tell them that as far as we were concerned the dispute goes on, and that Chobham Farm, midland cold storage and hays transport. The mass meeting that we held to celebrate the victory was held on Tower Hill which is adjacent to the Tower of London where so many people were beheaded or hung; I expect that Donaldson wished that he could have used the Tower.

As yet the trade unions had not delivered us one new job. We had through adopting a direct militant action delivered both container bases who had indicated that they were willing to employ registered dock labour; we estimated that there were some two to three hundred jobs that had been created as a result of our blacking and picketing campaign. We met several times to evaluate the situation and to discuss our next step, by that I mean where next to picket, it was to be this that split our committee completely into two groups. I belonged to a section of the shop stewards committee that represented the younger members, whilst the leaders of

Death of the Docks

our committee had the support and following of the more elderly section of our Industry. As with most groups of younger people they don't share the opinion of the gently, gently approach, and what was about to happen had been unthinkable a week ago. Also younger people do not tend to have unlimited patience's, we had after all waited years for the powers to be to get to grips with our problem, and, they hadn't done much in the way of getting us back our work. So with victory ours we sensed a killing. I tabled a resolution for the whole shop stewards committee to vote on, it read "that we start immediate action by picketing the London International Freight Terminal (the L.I.F.T), there were some fifteen hundred jobs at this depot, some of our shop stewards put the figure much higher, our chairman asked that any vote be deferred until our next meeting, we knew that they (the old school) didn't want to picket there.

I left the meeting wondering why we were meeting with such resistance to picketing a place that we could knock over in a few weeks, and ,create enough jobs to almost solve the problem of the "temporary" unattached register, that had been created by the ship-owners who where the owners of the very places that had caused the problem . The next meeting of the shop stewards threw up all the answers to my questions, as an alternative to picketing the L.I.F.T the chairman suggested that we picket a small container base just outside the docks called Woodcocks, at best it would deliver no more than20 jobs , we were flabbergasted ,the argument put forward by the supporters of this new idea was that it was small so therefore it would not pose the problems that picketing the L.I.F.T could pose, adding that other container bases on seeing Woodcocks being knocked over would not want a fight and would join the dock labour scheme voluntary. After someone had picked me up after I had been knocked over with shock, we proceeded to undo the feeble argument that had been offered as their presentation for picketing Woodcocks as opposed to the L.I.F.T .We asked if other container bases would meekly surrender on seeing Woodcocks being beaten, then why hadn't they already thrown in the towel after the scenes at Chobham Farm? It did not matter what we said or how good the argument that we presented we found ourselves knocking our heads against a brick wall. We asked for the vote to be taken, after 2 recounts the voting was tied.

We immediately asked for the matter to be discussed at the next meeting. That was the best we could get, the shop stewards who had been "defeated" were livid, it was they in the main along with the men who supported them that beat Chobham Farm, it was again they in the main that had done all the running around and the organising to get the 5 men released from prison.Come the next meeting both camps drafted in supporters to back their views, I had never seen such a well attended meeting, it seemed that every possible shop steward was in attendance, we went through the same arguments and cometh the vote we went under by the tinniest of margins. By now the men had got wind of what was going on inside the committees; the recriminations were flying about with both sides accusing each other of all sorts of things. One thing that most certainly emerged that was credible was that the communist party did not want the L.I.F.T. picketed, the communist party had a committee made up of industrial workers, to this day no one outside of the communist party has ever been given an explanation as to why they did not want us to picket the L.I.F.T., also they must have known how the issue was dividing our committee. I will never forgive the communist party for what they did. Also the Transport Union had a very large membership base inside the L.I.F.T container depot, so they never wanted

Death of the Docks

us to picket a depot where they had both sets of workers claiming the work to be theirs.

The Jones/Aldington enquiry was making headway and we heard that a report was being prepared to be delivered to both the minister and the dock delegate's conference. The rumours that were circulating were not good ones, all we could find out was that severance pay was to be increased, now if this was true then all our work would have been in vain. The T&G.W.U re-convened the docks delegate conference some three weeks after the same body of men had called us out on official strike, it became obvious that much arm twisting had gone on, the union had worked night and day on getting the delegates who had abstained to support the deal that the union was recommending to the conference. Everyone attending the conference as a delegate was given a copy of the final report of the Aldington/Jones recommendations to solve the current crisis in our Industry. It was not worth the paper that it was written on; we had been sold right up the river.

No words can describe the magnitude of the sell out that was about to take place. We had prior to the imprisonment of our members fought ourselves into a position of immense strength. But far be it for the trade union the use that strength during negotiations, in fact they had met daily and worked out a package that went nowhere near to the demands of the national port shop stewards committee, what the trade union had done could have been agreed with the shipping companies months ago, long before our men had taken the action that had turned the tables in our favour. Jack Jones had not only sold his birthright in securing and recommending this deal, but he would be instrumental in the killing of our industry. Although the union had gone to work on securing the delegates who had abstained, they left nothing to chance in making sure the deal would be accepted and it was Jack Jones himself who was to present the report to conference, something unheard of as the docks officers always conducted these conferences.

The trade union knew that all the major ports were against the deal, and to complicate matters further when dockers who were outside Transport House heard what sort of deal that Jones was recommending they burst into the hall where the conference was being held, now it wouldn't do for the union to bring in the police against their own members, so what do you do? All hell had broken out, and when our men heard that a vote had already been taken and the deal had been accepted by53 votes to30 that was it, delegates from non-scheme ports along with delegates who represented tiny amounts of men had swung the vote for the union. Jack Jones seeing the bitterness and anger in our men agreed to meet with them. He saw this as the only way of averting a full scale riot inside Transport House, so it was all upstairs to the large conference hall were Jack Jones would address our members. What he attempted to do in an effort to defuse the situation was to exchange small talk with men who were overawed by the occasion of the general secretary "having a laugh with them", this went down like a lead balloon, so he adopted a direct approach and proceeded to go on the attack.

Explaining that you don't always get everything that you want in negotiations',(he never had to tell us that). What surprised me was his approach in trying to justify why the union had recommended this filth, he never had what all good negotiators always have, that is a surprise that will always make someone stop and think he had nothing. Tempers became even more frayed and when one of our men hurled a large brass ashtray at Jack Jones, (it missed him by a whisker) we knew that we had to step in, we ushered him out while he was still screaming about louts and bully boys trying to intimidate people.(now doesn't that

Death of the Docks

sound familiar?). Jack Jones had been unable to answer our men's questions yet he had managed to get this agreement through. He repeatedly tried to assure us that far from being the end it was in fact the start of something new in the dock Industry, in fact he was so convincing in his argument, that all was not lost, and that he had you thinking that there must be something in it for us. After we had got rid of him we set about trying to calm our men down, we told them that we shared the same views as they did on the report and that we would be meeting to review everything. We met early on Friday morning to assess the situation, we had organised a mass meeting of our members, not to be held at our usual venue (the dock gates) but we hired the playing fields in Plaistow, these were enclosed and as such we could keep the press out.

By the time we were holding our mass meeting the majority of the other major ports had held theirs and most of them had voted to go back to work, we were really up against it, we had met earlier that morning before any decisions' had come through and as such we were recommending that we continue the strike, albeit on an unofficial basis. The only thing that the Jones/Aldington report had been positive about was that the severance pay was to be doubled, and that in London up to 1000 men could be released, (this being the size of the un-attached register), other ports would be able to release men depending on the labour requirements of individual ports. Most of our men had only ever dreamt of £4000, none of them had ever had £4,000 to their name, so this was another obstacle that we were confronted with. The men had heard the results of the other ports by the time that they started arriving for our mass meeting. As the saying goes "We were done for".

Our chairman and secretary both of whom had been imprisoned gave speeches which outlined our demands, stating how the Jones/Aldington report had delivered nothing of any substance, in fact yet again we had been offered a whole load of promises, they had wallpapered over the huge cracks in our Industry, Bernie Steers our secretary told the men that the document spelt disaster for us, unfortunately for us he wasn't saying what the men wanted to hear, they had come with their minds already made up. Nothing that our speakers could say was going to change their minds, short of offering them things that we couldn't deliver; we were on a hiding to nothing from our own men. When Vic Turner, our chairman called for the vote it was over whelming in favour of going back to work and not to resume any Industrial action on our own. This was the first time that the men had turned over the unofficial committee; many of our shop stewards did not know how to handle the situation as this was alien to all of us.

The Blame Game

So the T.&G.W.U had done us like kippers , we had delivered Barking container base and chobham farm, this was nearly 300 hundred jobs, the Jones/ Aldington enquiry had not only delivered any jobs but had increased the severance pay which would further reduce the already depleted labour force. From being in the strongest position that any unofficial committee could possibly be in, we now found ourselves trying to pick up the pieces, not only did we have that to contend with but we found ourselves being blamed by the elder statesmen of the shop stewards committee for being responsible for the current situation. When they were challenged as to their motives for not going ahead and picketing the L.I.F.T very little was offered as an excuse as to why we should not picket the L.I.F.T, and which in our opinion had we been allowed to it would have maintained the unity we enjoyed before it became the instrument that drove a wedge between us.   The communist parties response to all this was to remove all there delegates from the shop stewards committee, not only did they do that but they used their considerable influence that they had with the men ,trying to explain that it was the younger shop stewards who was responsible for any divisions.

So we had to elect a new chairman and secretary and start from scratch, the truth of the matter was that the real cause of our troubles were the T.&G.W.U, the depths that they stooped to in getting the picketing and blacking campaign ended, the union knew that by taking over our dispute that it would take the sting out of our tail. We had to weather the storm and soldier on knowing that our every move was being closely scrutinised by many groups.They (the older stewards) had refused to accept any criticism or that they had made a serious blunder in not picketing the L.I.F.T, now when the Industry faced its darkest hour they walked away from the unofficial movement, with many of them taking up posts within the union. After all what the trade union had done to us many of them chose to join ranks with them, claiming that you can only change within. A little late for that train of thought to be brought into play.

Another casualty of the Pentonville 5 was the local labour M.P Reg Prentice, because of his comments and opinions on the jailed dockworkers he was de-selected as the M.P for Newham North East, being the man of principles he was, he immediately joined the Conservative Party. How these toilets get away with it I'll never know, many other M.P s have switched sides mid-term , despite the fact that the electorate had elected them on the original "party ticket", principles? Don't make me laugh.

I'll tell you how over worked and underpaid these M.P s are, when our local M.P, Sir Elwyn Jones was made up to Lord Chancellor we had to select a new candidate to fight the bye-election, bearing in mind that candidates have to be nominated by trade union branches or the local wards of the labour party or the Co-operative movements we had 105 applications for the vacancy! And by all accounts this was not unusual. Although Prentice prolonged his stay in Parliament he eventually sunk without a trace.

So we (the younger Shop stewards) had been entrusted in running the unofficial committee, we knew we could never rise to the heights that we had recently witnessed, but we knew that the Industry was slowly bleeding to death through modernisation, and the people in the powerful jobs saw voluntary severance as the solution, what a load of crap. The truth was that they were dodging the issue and by regularly de-creasing the register strength they thought that they could put of solving today's problems until tomorrow. The T.&G.W.U had a brainstorm, they tried to get the Shop Stewards to sit on the committees and negotiate with the employers, this they said would remove any future conflict between the union delegates and ourselves, all very fine until you examine what we could and couldn't discuss, what they actually wanted was for us to be tied down with the bureaucracy that we were opposed to! So we decided "thanks but no thanks" to their magnificent offer, and we continued along the road that represented our men.

The first few mass meetings that the "new" committee called were sparsely attended, this being a direct result of rumours that were circulating as to why certain shop stewards never held the influential posts within the shop stewards committee, but as everyone knew we were fighters and not quitters, so it was tread softly until the men needed us, as if the job wasn't hard enough when we saw that the royal group of docks was the only dock in London who were continuing with the overtime ban, we asked the men if they wanted to resume working overtime when it was available, we always called for three tellers from the crowd to count the vote, this always ensured complete openness , but although I knew the vote was close, the three tellers would decide one way or the other, when the first one told me carried, the second one said he thought the vote was against, then the third one said that he thought it was a tie! I quickly declared the vote a tie and as such the overtime ban would remain in place until they voted it down.

We began meeting the port employers and suggesting to them how they could attract more work, not in the form of shipping but in the shape of groupage work, this was loading and unloading containers. The infrastructure was already in place and it wouldn't upset local communities who were having these bases imposed on their areas , with all the benefits that it would bring, such as heavy lorries using roads not equipped to handle them, noise and pollution in residential areas . We urged them to either bid for this work or at the very least bring the "cowboy" employers into the dock where the whole area was already set up for heavy Industry; it was like talking to the wall. The shipping companies and the stevedoring companies did not want to know.Jack Jones was still basking in his glory of settling up a dispute that never looked solvable , but not only had he "solved" it (I don't think so), but he had made a General Macarthur type speech in getting the men on his side. The bones of the thoughts of Chairman Jacks was that registered dockworkers had for the first time ever achieved job security, keeping a straight face, Chairman Jack went on by urging all registered dockworkers that coupled with the security the wage structure allowed dockworkers to go out and get a mortgage, the only part of Macarthur's speech that was missing was the immortal words "I shall return", maybe he was advised not to use the phrase! The words came back and haunted him on more than one occasion.

The national port shop stewards committee was still fully operational and was still as powerful as it had ever been, although we had been dealt a blow when Jack Jones wrested the blacking and picketing campaign we knew it was only a matter of time before the whole issue would rear its head again. When it did we could hardly believe who would be the next perpetrator to step forward and wield the axe.

Death of the Docks

Lord Vestey had spent a huge amount of money in converting one of the sheds in the Royal Victoria Docks, he had 4 huge conveyor machines built that would stretch from the shed right down into the ships hold, the dockworkers would place the frozen lambs into the conveyor where it would begin its journey from the ships hold into a lorry waiting on the quayside, this machine was equipped to read the mark on the lamb and despatch it to the appropriate lorry that was waiting for it. This was technology, the likes of that we had never seen, but in order to live with the modern world you had to you had to accept change. Also it was good that for the first time we had someone who was prepared to invest in our Dock. This was as it turned out to be the decoy of all decoys, Never having had millions of pounds to spend I Don't understand their thinking, but I take my hat off to Vestey in leading us up the garden path, and in doing it he spent a small fortune in misleading both us and the men.   We actually believed that if a leading player was prepared to invest huge sums of money in modernising the dock then perhaps we played a part in the future. The national port shop stewards committee seemed to be spending more time visiting Transport House in order to see Jack Jones about the rapid deterioration of our industry, we continually enquired as to where were the jobs that the Jones/Aldington enquiry had promised, and also how many non-scheme ports had been brought into the scheme. We already knew the answers to our questions, but it was for him to sit in his chair squirming and protesting that we had to give him a chance.

It was during one of these visits to see him when dear old Jack came out with a classic, it was after we had finished telling him of our intentions of calling all our members to mass meetings to bring them up to date with the lack of progress being made, we were all just in small groups exchanging small talk when our Jack came out with it "You're getting on my nerves, you don't know what I have to put up with when I meet the ship-owners, and if that's not bad enough you keep on slagging me off to the men" he then told me that perhaps I should try meeting the employers and get nothing from them and see how I like it. I told him that perhaps if he used the mighty strength that the union had on the odd occasion, then perhaps he would command some respect from the shipping companies, no one expected that the offer would be taken up so soon after our meeting with him.

The good Lord Vestey must have completed his programme of investing the money that our blokes had earned for him outside in container bases because out of the blue Vestey announced that the company he owned in the royal group of docks, Thames Stevedoring was to close with the loss of over 500 jobs, the usual garbage was rolled out about the company couldn't keep on sustaining the losses that they were at present, and that they had tried everything in their power to avoid it coming to this. The statement finished up by thanking the men for their years of loyal service. Sound familiar? I think that most companies pass this speech on to whoever is next for the chop. The national port shop stewards committee never hesitated in instructing us to approach Jack Jones and inform him that if these men were to be returned to the un-attached register then we would have no alternative other than to call an all out national dock strike.

This really tipped him over the edge, he again reminded us as to how the situation was difficult and complicated, the calling of strikes is not the answer, he then delivered a broadside, "I will call a meeting with Lord Vestey and the

Death of the Docks

P.L.A board and ill invite you along to see firsthand what they are like" Sure enough two days later I was told to attend a meeting at the World Trade Centre in St Katherine's Dock, the line up was pretty impressive, three general secretaries, the national and regional dock secretaries plus two delegates from the work peoples side who sat on the national joint council for our Industry not forgetting of course yours truly. On the Employers side we had two Lords, one being Lord Aldington plus the ever so nice Lord Vestey, with three knights of the realm thrown in for good measure, between the lot of them there wasn't a day's work in the lot of them.

Lord Aldington chaired the meeting, with Jack Jones leading off for the unions, his whole case seemed to be built around apologising for the current situation, he never once attacked Vestey for being the architect of the problem in the docks, the other trade union representatives' chimed in and the employers all sympathised with the problem but stated that there was little that anyone could do to offer a practical solution. This was rapidly developing into a mutual admiration society, at this point the only two people who had not contributed anything was Vestey and myself, just as Lord Aldington was about to close the meeting I asked if I could make my contribution, Lord Aldington stated that they welcomed everyone's viewpoint and asked me to proceed.

I thanked the good Lord and began by asking what was the Lord(Vestey) sitting on his left doing at the meeting, as he had not contributed a single word in the form of an explanation as to why he was throwing over 500 men on the scrap heap this Friday. I continued by challenging his right to be in attendance as it was he who had been responsible for the jailing of 5 of our men and that it was he who was largely responsible for building container bases and manning them with non-registered labour. I sympathised with the employers who would be left in the docks as it would be they who would have to bear the financial brunt of picking up the labour that Vestey was about to dump on them, I likened his attendance at this meeting as that of a murderer sitting and passing judgement on himself, then I took out of my pocket a piece of paper and read out the national port shop stewards decision to commence a national dock strike from 8 a.m the coming Monday.

This appeared to shake one or two of the employers, and Lord Aldington thanked me for my contribution adding that he had heard of me and was pleased to have the opportunity to meet me,(I don't think so),adding that he disagreed with nearly all of my views he went on by defending the integrity of one of his colleagues(Lord Vestey), adding that he and his family had contributed an immense amount towards the creation and helping employ vast numbers over the years, he also stated that he didn't like personal attacks directed at the good Lord, he did however thank me for being frank and honest and asked me what the national port shop stewards thought they could achieve by calling a strike. I thanked him for his kind words but again reminded everyone that as it was Vestey who was the cause of more trouble, then it should be him who paid everyman there full wages until such times as the men were found new permanent employment. A recess was taken at this point, during which I was accused of showing up our general secretary, I treated the remark with the contempt it deserved, informing the trade union delegation that if that was how they normally carried on then no wonder our Industry was in the mess that it was in. Agreement was reached very late in the day, the terms of the settlement were never made known to us, but who cared as long as our men were not to suffer because of the actions of the Vestey family. Whether or not the employers got Vestey to pay the men's wages until they had been found permanent employment was never revealed, but a

Death of the Docks

face saving deal yet again had been reached, with the same result of wallpapering over the cracks; however with the amount of employers left in the dock shrinking the cracks were becoming ever wider.

So what about the general secretary's famous statement that dockworkers had at last been given security and could for the first time ever take out a mortgage. The way that the trade union was allowing the docks to decline you couldn't take on a mortgage on the dogs' kennel, yet alone a home.

It was a short time afterwards that I was approached to see if I would consider becoming a full time paid officer of the union, the benefits were explained to me, they included a very low interest mortgage and a car supplied by the union plus various other benefits that made up a very nice package. It took me about 30 seconds to decline the offer, when asked why I would not consider the offer I told the "messenger" that my purpose was to assist the working class, not keep on telling them to get back to work or doing a deal that could only be described as selling out the men that they purport to represent.   Having declined the trade unions invitation to join the ranks of the privileged full time paid official I was approached some weeks later by my employer. He was not a great admirer of me; in fact he often told me how much he disliked both me and what I represented, so I never asked him to form a fan club for me. He then offered me a foreman's job not in his company but in Saudi Arabia! The offer was put to me in graphic detail and he told me that this was a golden opportunity to secure my future, the pay was £12,500 per year, tax free. Considering that we now earned a little under £2,000 per year before stoppages there was a vast difference. I wondered why I was being offered all these jobs. Perhaps I had gained a reputation of being a hard working conscientious person! Hmm. What I did know was that he never had my best interest at heart. So it was once again thanks but no thanks.

Although a deal had been reached that averted a strike, the position in the royal group of docks was becoming more serious, with the speeding up by shipping companies who were changing over to container ships from the old conventional ships that had used our docks, this was leading to men having no work, berths were frequently empty, and the enormous cold stores that were in the dock, that were large enough to store enough meat for the country in the event of a war were left to rot. The plan was beginning to take shape, why else would the Vestey Group build new cold stores when there were already plenty inside the docks? Yes after a century of meagre conditions and pitiful living conditions, just when the dockworkers were getting a rightful wage with better conditions the whole bloody thing was about to come crashing down on top of us.

What was happening was that as one employer was leaving it was placing a huge strain on the employers that were left. Jones/ Aldington's continued reaction was to keep on increasing the amount of men that could be released under the voluntary severance scheme, this had a double barrelled knock-on effect to the industry, firstly far from solving our problems it was steadily weakening us as the register strength was gradually de-creased, but again it would put an unbearable strain on port employers who remained as port employers, far be it for me to show any compassion towards port employers, but what was happening was that as the severance pay offer was being taken up, the bill was being met by a loan from the government and it would be re-paid through the national dock labour board. They recouped the money by increasing the levy that the employers paid to uphold and administer the scheme; this levy was already a bone of contention

Death of the Docks

with employers as non-scheme ports never had to pay such a levy giving them an unfair advantage over ports that belonged to the scheme.

So the port employers who remained in the Dock could be excused for feeling that they were being unfairly treated, in being forced to take the labour force that the good Lord Vestey and other employers who had jumped ship and abandoned the labour force. This was why since 1947 when the national dock labour scheme was introduced the shipping companies and the port employers wanted to be rid of the whole dock labour scheme, in fact it only emerged many years later that the Tories in the early seventies under the leadership of Ted Heath had appointed a secret committee to study and examine ways that they could remove the dockworkers registration, so secret was this committee that over ten years later the government still denied that it ever existed.What this committee apparently reported back to the conservative government was "that it would be unwise to make any attempt on removing the dockworkers registration as the trade unions do not have overall control of the membership, the crucial ports were in the hands of groups of communists and other extremist groups who the men follow" this tells you bundles about the trade unions.

We were not in the grip of a communist or Trotskyite take over, in fact I have explained to you that were it not for the actions of the communist Party we would still have an industry, what we meant to our men was that we listened to our members, we acted on behalf of our members. So if that places you in the "Extremist" bracket hard luck. To this very day I still fail to understand why Jack Jones remained on the Jones/Aldington committee, it appeared that there only regular function was to approach the government for extra cash so as they could both increase the amount of severance pay and to release more men from the register, no jobs had been forthcoming from this pair of mavericks, no non-scheme ports had joined the Scheme, so what was the point from a trade union viewpoint of remaining on board the"S.S.Hardluck"?What was apparent was that Jack Jones was getting fed up with the constant visits being made by the national port shop stewards to his den in Transport House, and the amount of telephone calls being made, all of a sudden he started to be unavailable on more and more occasions, we fully understood that "Our Jack" represented over 3 million members meaning that he just wasn't a dockers representative, but he was becoming a recluse when it come to seeing or speaking to us, how we know that he was dodging us was we telephoned him at Transport House and received the usual reply "Jacks away on business", we then got someone else to phone, the secretary asked who was calling and our man informed her that he was Ian Ross(no relation) the B.B.Cs Industrial correspondent , wallop! Straight through and a red faced general secretary had some explaining to do.

We had a Shop Steward who was gifted with amongst other things a knack of being able to impersonate anyone, so good in fact that had he chose to he could have made a living at it. He decided to impersonate Eamon Andrews who hosted what was then one of the most popular television shows this is your life. He phoned several of the leading lights, past and present and after getting an assurance of total secrecy from whoever he was speaking to, told them that the show was going to feature the life of Jack Dash, but again he told them that if one word was to escape then the whole show would be cancelled. The bait was taken, hook line and sinker, he then told them when the show was to be filmed, adding that they always did a secret rehearsal and that one of the participants' had kindly allowed the television company to use his home in rehearsing the segment where

Death of the Docks

Jack meets his old work chums. They were then informed to attend on that Saturday at mid-day, he then informed them that they could take a taxi as the studio would pay, adding that after the rehearsals had finished they would retire to the local pub! Sure thing that Saturday they began arriving by cab and when they realised that the whole thing was a sting they were not best pleased, so annoyed in fact that to this day no-one has ever owned up to being responsible.

My job as well as being a shop steward was also a "trouble shooter", this entailed attending any dispute in the docks were the local shop steward and employer could not agree over a dispute, I had been nominated by the trade union to do the job, with the employers supplying a representative so as the chairmanship rotated on a weekly basis. You had to hear both sides' present details of the disputed job and rule on an impartial basis. I was as impartial as the employers were when came to arbitrating, the employers complained to the trade unions about me, citing my behaviour as a shop steward and as arbitration chairman, now this was music to my ears, for if you are doing your job representing the men, then you don't expect any plaudits from the bosses.

Tom Wallis who was my employer also had stevedoring firms in the now defunct West India Docks and in Tilbury Docks, but by far the largest labour force was in the royal group of docks, now Tom Wallis was a canny type, it had been his father who had built the companies up when stevedoring contractors were earning fortunes, every dock would be bulging at the seams and when there was a lull in the work then his companies never had to pay anyone, this would be the responsibility of the N.D.L.B, so if ever the bosses wanted utopia this was it. Like many other employers, Tom Wallis never troubled us when the companies were earning serious profits, but the minute that he thought that his standard of living might be affected, and then he never hesitated in calling a meeting to try and squeeze a little more from the men. When we pointed out to him that he never called a meeting and offered the men a bonus when he was making huge profits, he tried like all the other port employers every conceivable trick that you could imagine. In fact sometimes they were so convincing, that not only did they believe the lies that they were telling but they almost had you believing them. If Oscars had been handed out to port employers for the best liar's category, it would have been almost impossible to split them.

The ship-owners were finding it very difficult to make the adjustment from an Industry where you had to literally slog your guts out to achieve a reasonable standard of living, to one where they had to pay you a decent wage regardless of how much work you done, or in their eyes much worse, as they had to pay you the wage even when there was no work for you to do. The strange thing about the whole situation was that the ship-owners and the port employers had entered into the new wage structure probably knowing that containerisation would decimate the amount of shipping that would steam up the River Thames to be unloaded. The employers, unlike us knew what modernisation would bring, while we had, had to try and visualise what modernisation would do to the once booming and vibrant docks, they were fully aware of the consequences that containerisation would bring to the Industry.

Ship-owners like all other major employers plan years ahead whilst the workers and their representatives look no further than the next wage packet, this was what gave the employers the edge over us, just try and convince the men when the docks are busy that in six months or in a years' time there will be no work, they would have you certified!

You pay your union subscriptions with a view that the trade unions will secure you a good working agreement,

Death of the Docks

with fair wages and conditions thrown in as a bonus. But, what you do expect your trade union to do for you is to defend your livelihoods and to be able to warn you of any impending perils. I Don't think that this is asking too much of the mighty T.&G.W.U, who along with the labour party boast of one of the finest research centres. It seems that the research into containerisation got lost at sea.

During the summer of the great drought I was working in a shed delivering cargo onto the lorries that the importer would send to collect his cargo. This particular day I was working with Alan Williams, we had done practically nothing and as it was approaching our dinner break we decided to call it a day, we parked up the fork lift truck and just as we were leaving the shed the foreman called us back. A lorry had arrived to collect a huge load of hay that had been imported from Canada because most of ours had not grown due to the weather. We informed the driver that we would load him when we returned from dinner, load me now and I'll give you a good tip.Seeing an opportunity to get ourselves a nice few bob we launched ourselves into loading this hay onto his lorry. We just made it when it comes to settling up with us he casually told us the name of a horse! Back this horse when it runs in a 3 mile handicap. He had done us. We waited 3 weeks, scouring the racing pages of the newspapers everyday to see if the horse was running in the race he indicated, sure enough it was running and exactly as the driver had predicted, our gang had a collection and we absolutely lumped on it, it's still running. The moral being when it's your lunch break take it

THE LAST RITES

To attend a dockworkers funeral is another experience that shouldn't be missed,(unless it's your own) they like most other people pay their respects at the house or the cemetery, usually it would be at the cemetery, which would generally have a pub near the gates where everybody would meet up before the hearse and cars following arrived. It was at a funeral of a friend of my Dads that I really saw how the departed are sent off in true Dockland fashion! The funeral was for one of the Docks real characters, his nickname was" Orrible", and I don't have a clue as to how he acquired the name, but everyone referred to him as Orrible, I must add that Orrible was a perfectly normal bloke, a little gruff but generally speaking a very decent person. But he was Orrible to everyone. He had been a Tally Clerk for the best part of his life and was very well known and respected, and as such the better known that you where the bigger turnout you got at your funeral, anyway for Orribles funeral there was a grand turn out, and after we had a couple of pints in the nearby tavern we all left the pub to stand inside the grounds for the arrival of the hearse.Everyone was keeping an eye out for the cortege, and it seemed that the funeral was running late, the vicar who was to officiate at the service appeared out of the crematorium to see where the funeral was, the vicar had a white cloak draped over his shoulder, this resembled the backing cloth that we used when we

Death of the Docks

were backing chilled beef, one of our blokes said to the vicar "you had better disappear, if old Orrible sees you he won't show up because he wasn't too fond of doing beef". The vicar didn't see the funny side. Relations never improved when another mourner told the vicar "he was always late for work so I suppose there's no point in expecting him to be on time for his own funeral "

The best always came out afterwards when everyone would have a drink, stories relating to the person who had passed on would be recalled, as the beer flowed the stories would become funnier, in fact you could have been mistaken for not thinking that you were not at a funeral at all, the person whose funeral that you may have attended would usually be put into one of two classes, if you where a quiet sort of person who just minded his own business and always tried hard to find work, you belonged to the group whereby you were best summed up as "a greedy b------d," where as if you followed the unofficial committee and always stood up for your rights you would fall into the group that consisted of people who where " lazy communist b-------d". You can't win, even when you're dead! But rest assured you could always be assured of a decent send off! Tragically as I got older I noticed that at each funeral there were less and less attending funerals, this was because the" olduns " numbers were decreasing at a rate of knots, meaning that at each subsequent funeral there were less characters around. We also noticed that with the drive to get more men to accept voluntary severance that it was removing most of the characters from the dock, not only where these men characters but they where our hardiest supporters whenever we needed support, the register strength was decreasing at a speed that was not giving out the right signals for the future of our Industry.

We bombarded Jack Jones and any dock officers in the unions, who would listen, but listening is one thing, doing something about it is another thing. So dear old Jack, desperate to get us of his back arranged for a meeting-come conference to be held, everyone who was anyone in the dock industry was to be in attendance, Jack Jones made it his first priority to ensure that the shop stewards from every firm in London's remaining Docks were to be invited. The theme of the conference was the future for the Port of London, and for the changing handling methods that containerisation would bring about. Tagged on the end of the agenda was the security that the Introduction of modern handling methods would bring to the registered dockworker, now this if nothing else would be interesting. All the big hitters from the port employers were there along with all the senior trade union officials, the "star" turn was to be John Peyton who was the Minister of Transport, thus making him responsible for our Industry.

No expense had been spared in organising the seminar, fleets of coaches to take everyone to another venue for lunch, and then to bring you back for the finish of the seminar, glossy brochures showing how the Port of London along with the workforce would still be in business for many years ahead, with the underlying theme being ,together we will both benefit from the modern handling techniques! Perhaps I had been missing something, still it promised to be interesting.Like most seminars the early speakers were both boring and liars, still the best was to come after lunch when all the big hitters would be giving us the wisdom of their expertise, the anticipation of all of this seemed to make a few of our blokes a little nervous, and as such while taking lunch they gave the wine that was supplied on each table a terrible caning, so much so that they run out of the stuff! Back to the seminar and Jack Jones stated in his contribution that the Port of London Authority would be

Death of the Docks

the major employer in the future, and that given they make the right amount of investments then the future for the Registered Dockworker was a secure one.

The Chairman of the Port of London Authority followed ,and he outlined the P.L.A s determination to be a big player in the field of containerisation, with Tilbury being described as the new Rotterdam, but his speech was generally much the same as the one that Jack Jones had made only it had been shuffled about a bit.Then the star turn stood up to deliver his speech, he could barely be understood as his speech was a little slurred, but after waffling on about nothing of any importance he came out with a corker, to prove to everybody that he cared and was knowledgeable about the Industry he proudly announced" when I am in my ministerial office I have a dockers hook on one of the shelves, next to it there is a model of a fork lift truck, I look at these two objects and I think to myself that's progress!" With that he sat down, even the employers and the people who supported him were astounded and there was a long pause before any realised that he was finished. The whole thing was a farce, speaker after speaker told us that the future only held good fortune for us, you could have been forgiven in thinking that you had just crossed the palm of a fortune teller in a seaside booth, the only bit they left out was that we would meet a tall dark handsome stranger!

When it came to question time the whole thing erupted into a farce, the chairman did everything in his power to avoid taking a question from any of the shop stewards, when after we had demanded to be allowed some questions he took one or two and invited anyone to reply, when the question was posed "would the P.L.A consider along with government support in turning the royal group of docks into a huge groupage depot". This really threw the "chiefs" on the platform, after they had looked appealingly at each other in the hope that someone else would reply to the question the chap who was conducting the question and answer session came to their rescue, he stated quite forcibly that the question was being ruled out of order as the seminar had not been called for that topic, he then must have gained instant promotion by declaring that no more questions would be taken from our area as we had monopolised the session and other people wanted to put questions.In fact far from monopolising the question and answer session we had purposely been ignored, I suppose the chairman was under orders. He then took one more question and duly closed the meeting. We thanked Jack Jones for getting us an invitation and asked that if there were to be any more seminars or conferences', would he make sure that we were not invited. The whole thing had been a shambles and a complete waste of time.

However despite all our legitimate protests about the way that our Industry was slowly being bled to death by containerisation, and the spin offs that came with it we did not seem to be able to rekindle the movement to its previous heights, no matter that the men knew that the biggest Industrial massacre was taking place, they never had the heart for a battle, they knew that the next fight would be a fight to the finish, and with the whole system stacked against us they chose to duck the final showdown. Yet with the victory that had been pulled off in getting the men released was and will always be one of the greatest working class victories of all time.Coupled with this you had to throw in that the docks where known for not ducking an issue, if it meant having a fight then let's get on with it, this was the reputation that had been built up ever since the great strike of 1889.

Death of the Docks

One of the biggest contributing factors for the fact that the dockworkers were avoiding the final showdown was that the severance pay had robbed us of many of our supporters; it seemed that many of the "mainstays" had opted for the severance pay, leaving us without our hardcore supporters. Also throw in for good measure the communist party's new approach of sulking and seeming to take great pleasure to see if the "schoolchildren" (this was the name that they had given us)who took their places had made a mistake. Yet despite all of these obstacles the shop stewards committee began to get stronger as the time went on, but you can't help thinking that the time to arrest the situation had cost us dearly. What I really think frightened the trade union and the government was the way in which the shop stewards committee organised the entire work force to help out the miners, they had just gone into dispute with their employers and the government, the dispute had all the hallmarks of being a long and nasty affair. With the country being put on a 3 day week and electricity rationed leaving much of the country plunged into darkness most evenings via a power cut, the media had a field day with the miners, they were described as enemies of the country, but when the public opinion continued to grow in supporting the Miners the media was at a loss, the British public had always had a soft spot for the miners. Despite the onslaught from the media and people having no electricity night after night, despite the whole nation being put on a 3 day week the public wanted the miners to be settled up, the way most of the population viewed the dispute was that they would not want to have to do what miners did for their living, the job was dirty, dangerous and arduous. Both the press and the government had miscalculated the situation.

However the miners faced intense hardship if they were to win, and our shop stewards met and decided to help them financially, what we undertook was a mammoth operation in organising it, we never gave this amount of work a second thought, we called mass meetings to get our ideas accepted by the men, what we were proposing was that every registered dockworker contributes 25 pence a week until the dispute ends. The men readily accepted this and we swung our organising skills into overdrive.

The money that we collected would not be going to the miner's trade union (N.U.M) instead we would take it directly to the nearest pit to us; this was Betts hangar colliery in Kent. We wanted the money to be distributed to the striking miners who got no help from the state, single men being one of the many groups who were expected to live on fresh air. The task of collecting everyone's 25 p was not as difficult as we had expected, when everyone rallies round the task becomes that much easier, and by the first Friday we had collected £500,we were quiet pleased with this amount as it was our first week and we never quiet knew what to expect, we made contact with the area president of the N.U.M and told him that the money was to be distributed directly to the striking men, at the time of contact with them we never knew how much we would collect. Anyhow we made arrangements to travel to the pit and meet some of the local strike committee. That Friday night 4 of us set out to go to Deal in Kent to give them the money. We did not want any fuss; just a receipt and an assurance as to where the money would go. If you don't mind we had the cash in a carrier bag! The Kent area president was summoned when the miners heard how much we had collected, and that it was to be a weekly arrangement.

We were taken to their social club and at first we were being given some strange looks, but once the president arrived he stopped the band playing and made an announcement as to who we where and how much we had brought, when he told them that it was to be given every week and it was to go directly to strikers the whole

Death of the Docks

club erupted into cheers and applause. I am not easily embarrassed but that night I went as red as a beetroot, to top everything of it seemed that every miner in the place wanted to buy us a drink! We explained to Joe Burke, the area president that not only did we not come down for a booze up, but we certainly did not want to take drinks from strikers, he laughed as he told us that no one pays their bar bill until the strike ended! I along with our other stewards left the miners club quite tipsy and each week we sent different people with the money! In all we collected and handed over £1,500, and after the dispute had been successfully concluded the miners presented us with a miner's lamp as a token of their appreciation for all the help that the dockworkers had shown. We had very slowly built up the shop stewards movement into what could best described as an honest and straight forward committee, we were just finding our feet when Wham, the local committee of the T.&G.W.U rode into town and called the men out on strike in an effort to get the work back that had gone elsewhere, now you can call me naive but hadn't the issue been dealt with in 1972?

I usually could read industrial situations but this had caught me stone cold. Some years later it emerged that during both major strikes that we had been engaged in, the continuity rule strike in 1967 and the picketing and blacking campaign of 1972, which led to the unofficial strike and then the 3 weeks official strike, the C.I.A and the British equivalent M.I.5, where being supplied with details on various members of the unofficial committees who where leading the strikes. No I have not taken a funny pill or am suffering from a bout of being paranoid, no, when the official papers were released showing a Brian Nicholson as their informer he tried to laugh of the matter by insisting that he had fed them false information .The fact of the matter is if why you in are contact with the M.I 5 in the first place? What normal person has the secret service as bedfellows? Who was the Chairman of the No. 1Docks Group Committee? Yes you've got it Brian Nicholson! It was he who was to lead the strike! Why after all these years had the committee who had always been an obstacle to us and more importantly the men , decided to venture into an unofficial strike? But why did they sacrifice London? The men leading the strike had full and unfettered access to all the national dock committees within the union, so why commence a strike with just London?

The answer to this question could only be that they had tried to get national support and failed. Or was the strike called because the hierarchy of the T&G.W.U feared that the shop stewards movement was rising up again? This is my belief as some of the people who orchestrated this strike could be trusted no further than you throw them. Sadly none of these questions will ever be answered; the No. 1 docks group committee had always been a right wing union minded committee, but since the communist party members had withdrawn from the running of the shop stewards committee they and their supporters had taken up positions within the trade unions, so the most so-called "senior" shop stewards were now on the most influential union committees. But to call out London dockers on their own was suicidal to say the least. The media had a field day, although with just London spearheading the strike it never caused as much impact as a national stoppage would have caused, so the strike was relegated to minor items on the news bulletins', but at least the "senior" delegates cum shop stewards had the opportunity to prove that they could do the ground work without depending on us. In fact what transpired was that far from assisting our cause in getting back our work, they knocked the last remnants of

Death of the Docks

any stuffing out of our men, furthermore the perpetrators' of this suicidal venture never had the appetite for doing all the leg work, neither did they have willing workers to do it for them, this was a direct result of the people who were capable of doing this never trusted them.

What the media seized on was that Nicholson was out sick as a result of an accident, they accused him of expecting the men to forego their wages while he received benefits, this never worried us unduly as it wasn't his fault that he was out sick when he was asked to lead a strike, what concerned me was that 4 of the delegates who sat on the No. 1 docks group committee represented no docks at all, the area that they represented had long gone but knowing that they would not get automatically elected at a new trade union branch they kept their branches operational, thus letting them sit on all the powerful committees. To say the strike had caught me cold would be the understatement of the year, I had just under gone a very strange experience with my local labour party (I was still a member then) I needed rehousing as the maisonette that we lived in was a council estate full of problem families (perhaps the local council thought that my family were a problem family), the grief that my wife and children were getting was becoming unbearable. I had to do something as I was normally away a large proportional of the time on shop stewards business, and it wasn't fair on my wife.

So I approached my local councillor and asked for an exchange or another offer of a property that was not made up with every problem family in Newham, he arranged for the chairman of the housing committee to visit my home to discuss my problem. It was during the visit that I twigged as to what was going on, it was a well known fact that Newham council was run by freemasons, they were referred to as the square, holding all the important posts on the council, when I finally tumbled what was being offered to me I exploded, the going rate then to get a 3 bed roomed council house was £250, instead of keeping quiet and exposing them I went berserk ,I explained that all my life I had attempted to help people and had never sought or taken any form of bribe. I reminded them that they reminded me of the characters in "The Ragged Trousered Philanthropist", I must have worried the life out of them as I received a visit from another councillor informing me that I had gotten hold of the wrong impression, adding that the council would give me a 100% mortgage, so I was told that I should find a house within the borough and leave the rest to the treasury department of the council. Guilty consciences?

So when Nicholson and his band of merry men called us out on strike I hadn't long been in our new house, and because of a mix up with the local authority I found myself owing 3 months mortgage, now I don't recommend this. Luckily for me my father was no longer in the same boat as me and was able to help us out. But what really astounded me was that although we were isolated the men remained steadfast, this was heading to be the defeat of all defeats, and what's more whatever chances the shop stewards had of having a final roll of the dice had just disappeared. Port after port turned down the request of joining in the struggle, perhaps it had something to do with the leadership. These people leading us into oblivion were the same group of people who voted for every aspect of the modernisation programme, they were the same people who had condemned out of hand nearly every unofficial strike; they were firm believers in going through the official line. So why were they leading an unofficial strike? They had as much experience of leading and conducting a strike as a nun had arranging the annual beano (a glorified booze up), yet here they were leading a strike against everything that they had agreed! What they had as an advantage that

Death of the Docks

we never enjoyed was the t&g.w.u never called meetings to undermine them. I wonder why.

No attempt what so ever as being made to tackle the root cause of our problems, perhaps if the leaders of the strike had organised a mass demonstration outside a container base it might have convinced a few more people that the leaders of the strike were genuine in their attempt at this latest farce in trying to re-claim our work. The same people who were running this strike had participated on nearly every major committee that oversaw our Industry, it was they who negotiated the voluntary severance terms that was decimating our industry, and when the return to work from this debacle takes place you could be sure that there would be flood of fresh applications would be made. When the inevitable did take place and a return to work was underway the media seized on it as one of the most crushing defeats of all time, the morale of our men was at its lowest in living memory, I think most of the men were ready for a full course with the Samaritans, the last remnants of any fight had been crushed.

The only salvation that the shop stewards committee had was that the debacle wasn't of our making, however this was scant consolation. It wasn't the No.1 docks group who were left to pick up the pieces, this was down to us, and as sure as little acorns grow into giant oaks the flood of applications for voluntary severance almost reached saturation proportions. The men not only never saw any future but felt that the whole issue was a lost cause. So it was once more down to us to sort out the mess again, before the latest debacle the national register had plummeted down to less than 34,000. How many more of our members would seek "the pot of gold" remained to be seen. To best describe our plight you could liken it to a football team being 4-0 down with 5 minutes to go, the glass was definitely half empty now.

Another rumour that was doing the rounds was the Union, albeit via the No.1 docks group committee, had cooked up the dispute to prevent the shop stewards committee from regaining the high ground, the shop stewards would have organised the dispute nationally, this being the only way that our men stood a chance of beating the ship-owners. So, no sooner had we rebuilt the unity in the docks when the whole show was to tumble down around us. The strike had been suicidal; all that it had achieved was the probability of speeding up any proposed closures, although this was still being strenuously denied by everyone outside of the shop stewards movement. For the first time in my life I experienced the mood of our men had radically changed, the men had an air of expecting the worse, it was very difficult to try and explain the atmosphere that was evident in the docks, for the first time ever I was witnessing seasoned, hardened and good men resigned to accepting the inevitable, even if you spoke to the most optimistic men they told you that there was nothing that we could do to stop the closures or the speed up of the modernisation programme.

Men who had never considered taking the redundancy money where now giving serious thought to it. Two men who had taken the redundancy money, managed to get a job as hospital porters, over a glass of beer they told me how they were getting on. Part of their job was to remove the bodies of patients from the wards when they had passed away. Now part of their team was a young lad who was as flash as you like, whatever they said to him he just shrugged his shoulders, telling them "I've done that "or that he had a bigger one than you, no matter what conversation you were holding he would upstage you by dismissing what

Death of the Docks

you where talking about by declaring that he had done it, been there or that his one costs more than yours. Everyone was fed up with him but as he was a bit of a bully they were a little apprehensive of him, not our 2 blokes!

Another part of their job when they removed the dead bodies to the mortuary was to list any jewellery that the deceased person might be wearing, one of our chaps laid on the mortuary slab and covered himself with the sheet, the other one asked the flash Harry if he would nip down and record any jewellery that the new dead body might have on him. Knowing that he was a little frightened but not wanting to show it our bloke asked if he would be alright doing the task on his own. Apparently new dead bodies react in some strange ways, but flash Harry could not show any weakness so of he toddled to the mortuary.

When he arrived he walked round the dead body a few times then began to whistle nervously, finally he flicked part of the sheet to see if the body had a watch on, he now had to summon up the courage to remove the sheet from the dead bodies head to see if there was a chain around the neck, another few trips around the table but by know he was talking to himself, when he reached across to lift the sheet the body began to sit up and a loud moan emerged. This was too much for Flash Harry; he disappeared through the doors and never came back. He didn't even work out his notice. "The bigger they are, the harder they fall". This type of story could be retold a thousand or more times as our men found employment after they had left the docks, many of their new employers were quietly pleased with the ex-dockworkers that they had given a job to, Dockers never needed to be told what to do, they just sized up the job and got on with it. As 1976 rolled in so did another crisis, the employers sensing outright victory after recent events declared that the Port of London was carrying a surplus of labour; the few remaining employers issued a statement declaring that they estimated there was 1,250 men surplus to requirements.

Although the shop stewards knew the answer to the claims of the labour surpluses there was nothing that we could do. The men did not want to hear anything that might cause more trouble; they had heard all the stories over the past five years or more about what the employers had got up to, they had heard all our talk of how the problem could be resolved. The unions seemed to be joining in with the lets be depressed mood, for after the abortive attempt that had been made, the unions had copped the blame, and they never needed much of an excuse to hide from trouble so they went on the missing list when it come to doing anything. When you did finally manage to corner a union delegate they hid behind the recent debacle, so they blamed the men for losing the strike that they had led! Heads you win Tails I lose. You could say that the whole dock had become candidates for the Samaritans. As you are probably aware when you are down in the dumps you don't make rational decisions, this was also reflected in the mood of our men, if you're feeling really hacked off then in a moment of weakness you think to yourself I can escape all of this and get myself a few grand and get another job. This was how many of our members applied for the severance pay.

The Aldington/Jones bandwagon rolled back into town to discuss episode 34 of the crisis in the docks, you understood where Lord Aldington was coming from, and where he and the whole group of employers associated with our Industry where bound for, but what was Jack Jones playing at? Couldn't he or the big players in our union see what was happening to our Industry? History will show that the Aldington/Jones committee were set up to deal with the problem of dock work. Their idea of dealing with the problem was on a similar footing on how the Americans

Death of the Docks

dealt with the Red Indians. Wipe them out and the land is ours!

I was interviewed for an article in the employers newspaper" The Port," during the interview I did for the article I suggested that as there were a lot of men going home each day with no work, then perhaps the employers should give serious consideration to using the spare labour more wisely , they had empty sheds and the machinery that was laying idle doing nothing, and I suggested that they start putting out tenders on a very competitive basis to get groupage work into the docks. The reasoning behind my suggestion being was that if you attract the work by offering to do it cheaper than the people outside, then once you got the work established then the employers could gradually increase the price. But the thinking behind the suggestion was to get our men and our industry back to full capacity again. The furore that the article caused beggars belief; it was not the unions that I had upset but the London port employers and their chums the shipping companies, it was left to my employer Tom Wallis to phone me and launch into a tirade of abuse towards me, accusing me of publicly accusing the employers of not knowing how to manage their own businesses. Continuing the barrage of abuse he accused me of helping the competitors of the port employers and he finished off by telling me to keep out of business that I didn't understand. I found myself in defending the article that I had written, that I was speaking and acting like the employer, I quickly gave him some travelling instructions and told him where to go. I was fully expecting to be arrested for committing treason! But this again proves that the major employers were not at all interested in bringing work into the docks.   No matter how many solutions that we come up with to deal with the problems, the employers didn't want to know. Ask yourself why, if you were experiencing financial difficulties and someone offered you advice on how to improve your situation would you ignore the help being offered? If someone offered you a solution to your problems then you would bite their hand off to accept it... unless you had ulterior motives.

Back to Jack Jones and his crony Lord Aldington and what did they come up with? Yes you've guessed it, increase the voluntary severance pay; back they went to the government cap in hand for more money to support the severance programme. Let me ask you another very simple question, if you had 3 or 4 children all at work and contributing to the running of the house, gradually as they left home you never reduced your outgoings, but in order to replace the lost income you kept on taking out loans, how long then before the whole show comes tumbling down?Once again there was another mighty rush for the improved severance pay. The other major ports were all experiencing identical problems and when the national port shop stewards met the talk was all about how low the morale was in most ports. However as always our attitude was nothing but positive and we plugged on in the hope that we would get the break that we so badly needed to kick start our campaign.

Severance parties were becoming a common occurrence, with some parties being better than others. For some when they had done there last days work in the docks ,a glass or two of beer with their workmates was the order of the day before setting of home to face whatever the future could throw at you. But when one of the characters of the docks was leaving it would usually involve a full scale party, sometimes when one or two where leaving together then they would hold a collective wake, some of these parties were grander than some weddings that you attended.

Death of the Docks

One severance party that I attended was held in the dockers social club, scruttons maltby, they were one of the last remaining port employers in the royal group of docks, they were also one of the largest employers in terms of the amount of men they employed. The social club was a large spacious place where you could enjoy a beer after work, well this party was in full swing, a D.J had been engaged but because he couldn't find records from the 1950s he was given a drink and told not to bother by playing boom boom records! The poor bloke didn't know what was going on, instead of the records out came the piano, a pianist took the stage and the party really commenced, however despite the fact that several hundred pounds had gone into the till, the club steward , who was an ex docker, called time.

It was 3 o/clock in the afternoon, this being before the introduction of all day drinking. It was a known fact that you could get afters in the dockers club, especially when there was a big severance party, but the steward seemed to be in a bad mood and that was that, the only concession he would make was that we could buy a few cases of beer and drink them in the lounge room. This we had to do, as there was a television in there and afternoon horse racing was on it was time for the form pundits to take over, a quick check on how much was left in the kitty and the whole lot was despatched to the nearby bookmaking shop, the manager of the betting shop must have wondered what hit him, for coupled with the effect of the drink making you fearless and the purple patch that our tipsters had hit ,after three bets we were £500 up, this was a bloody fortune then but after a vote it was decided to put the lot on the next selection, the horse went and won.Now the celebrations really began, when the club steward returned he told us that we could return to the main bar, he was informed that we were all going to the local pub to complete the celebrations, I don't remember leaving the pub but I was informed that the party went on all night! The luck that we had was an exception to the rule, many dockworkers homes and lives had been ruined as a result of gambling. Some wives had to resort to visiting the docks on pay day to attempt to get some housekeeping money before the husband visited the local bookies.

But despite everything there were still many lighter moments that livened up proceedings, we were loading a ship for the Far East, this particular operation was that the pallet of cargo would be lowered into the ships hold by the crane for the fork lift truck to take it and stow it. Much of the cargo was confectionary and the fork lift truck driver had gotten himself a couple of bars of chocolate, one member of the gang kept going up to the fork lift and pinching the chocolate from the truck driver. The fork lift truck driver was getting really hacked off as there were literally thousands of bars in the cargo so why pinch mine? The next day just before we knocked off someone replaced the chocolate on the fork lift with some e-lax. Sure enough our old mate appeared and ate as much as he could. The next day he failed to show up for work! We had to carry him (this means you do his work between you and he still gets paid) when he finally showed up he told us that that night he went home and messed the bed, he and his wife changed all the bedding he had a shower and returned to bed, another searing pain and he leapt out of bed rushing downstairs to make the toilet, he fell down the stairs messed himself again and hurt his back! We never had the heart to tell him the truth and he still believed that it was something he had eaten in his tea break. Still we had to carry him for 4 days-so who was the joke on?

THE FINAL HUMILIATION

The next chapter of my life and that of the dock history is probably the saddest times of my life. For despite the fact that I had always represented our men with honour and dignity, and had shared with them moments of great successes in victories and the lows when we tasted defeat, I never sold out, I never sought favour or reward for what I had done, unlike some others who purported to be raving left wingers but had secretly amassed monies and properties, I did it because I got a great deal of satisfaction in helping the underdog beat the employer.

Despite several vain attempts to get the groupage work brought into the docks, we had known for years that if there was to be a future for our industry then it was groupage work that was the only hope that we held, but the shipping companies had absolutely no intention of using either the docks or registered labour to carry out this work. Coupled with this you had the largest employer, and the owner of all the docks and the enormous amount of surrounding land the Port of London Authority seemingly not too worried about the whole situation. I suppose if I held huge amounts of land to sell then I wouldn't worry too much. The men seemed to be out of work more than they were in work, now you don't have to have a degree in economics to understand that this could not continue, the berths in the docks were empty more than they were occupied, then the Port of London Authority announced that as a cost cutting exercise they would "mothball" the Royal Victoria Docks. The domino effect was beginning to kick in, with the remaining employers having to absorb the labour discarded by port employers who had turned it in. Not only was our labour force being decimated but the docks were being to shrink.

Yet despite the perilous position the remaining employers were in, still they refused to obtain alternative work, so the only conclusion that you conclude is that all parties from the employer's side had full access to what plans were in store for the future of the docks, the value of the land was to be our downfall. The amount of land that was available to be developed when the docks were closed could quiet easily absorb a whole new town. I suppose the ship owners and the government saw the impending battle with us as a war, and if you gradually reduce the enemies' strength then when it comes to the final push the whole thing is easier, and our numbers had been seriously depleted through the severance scheme. All the port employers who had thrown the towel in up to now had always given the appropriate notice, however all this was about to end with the demise of the company where I worked T. Wallis(Royal Docks) Ltd. There had been a noticeable drop of the amount of work that we used to do; this had led to a marked increase in the men being sent home on full pay. Why this was happening all of a sudden no one knew, but what we did know was that it wasn't sending out the right signals. However our Tom wasn't a defeatist and he pulled a ship in for discharging. The ship had come from Pakistan, where it had loaded animal hoofs and horns, plus cattle skins with an assorted variety of other obnoxious cargoes. The men called me in to resolve a difference between them and the company, when I enquired as to what the problem was the gang invited me

Death of the Docks

to join them in the ships hold, just as I was about to get on the ladder that led you down into the ships hold someone warned me to watch out for the rats. Now I don't like rats, and that's the finish of it, so I called down to the gang that if they wanted me to resolve their dispute then they had better come up on deck and explain the facts to me. The gang explained to me that the entire hold was running alive with rats, not your run of the mill rat, these were bloody enormous rats, and I told them to knock off while the port health people were summoned. The port health inspector closed down the ship for 24 hours while the ships hold was fumigated.

After all the experts had given the all clear our men resumed unloading the remaining cargo. All that remained to be unloaded was about 1500 hessian bags of cattle cake, the bags that remained in the ships hold were stacked three high right across the entire area of the ships hold, and beneath the cargo was the ships floor (strangely enough this is called the ceiling), the men had only just resumed unloading the remaining bags when I was called back in. By now the Ships foreman was absolutely livid, the ship had been taken on a time charter and any overrun would incur penalties. He told me that there was no sign of any rats, but the men working the cargo told a different story they told me that the whole cargo was moving, caused by the amount of rats underneath it! The ships foreman started to climb down to the bottom of the hold and all the time he was assuring me that there was no rats, as he neared the bottom I spotted a huge rat climbing the ladder, when he saw it he leapt of off the ladder onto the cargo, needless to say the ship was taken out with the remaining cargo still aboard.

That summer I was reporting for work when the superintendent of the company told me that the governor wanted a word with me, he almost pushed me up the flight of stairs that led to his office, he then handed me the telephone. Tom Wallis was on the other end and he calmly informed me that the receivers were in ,adding that it was all over and would I thank the men on his behalf for all the service they had given! Tragically he was deadly serious; I told him where to go and what he should do to himself, but what was more tragic was that he had planned the bankruptcy, and the only people who were going to get hurt was us and a long line of creditors. Because dockworkers were not covered by the employment protection bill, we were not guaranteed to receive any monies owed to us by the parasite of an employer we had.

The meeting of the creditors was a cosy little set up, they all gathered in a hall in the City of London, with the prince of thieves(our former employer) who had robbed us of our wages sat on the raised platform with the receiver, this made us creditors and as such we had to be informed of the meeting. The receiver opened the meeting and asked if it could be adjourned, this by all accounts is par for the course, however the true account of what the carnage that Wallis had caused was emerging. We all paid a subscription towards the trade union hospital, Manor House hospital did a wonderful job for our members and their wives, and it relied solely on trade union members subscriptions to survive, Tom Wallis had stopped our subscriptions through the wage packet and had kept the last 6 months of our payments. Then you had the men who saved an amount of cash every week through there wage packet to save it up for your holidays or Christmas, this was then transferred to your Post Office savings account, the leader of the Robber Barons had stopped all your savings and kept them. Merry Christmas Tom. Then there was the small matter of our national insurance contributions', again the grim reaper of Bexleyheath had stopped our contributions' and spent them.

Death of the Docks

I objected to the meeting being adjourned, I was desperately looking to see if the trade unions or there solicitors where going to join the attack, but they hadn't showed up, so I launched into Wallis with all guns blazing, after explaining what he had done to our members I requested that the serious fraud squad be informed of what he had done. This isn't cricket, the establishment all rally to protect their own and despite the fact that he had robbed me of some £230, I received a cheque for 68 pence in full and final settlement. Many more of our men lost far more than I did. Had you or me attempted to do what he had just done they would throw the book at you, after they had locked you up and thrown away the key. But its only money, what was about to happen would have far more reaching effects on me than anything else that has ever happened to me in my life.

We had warned the powers to be that the unattached pool was never to be allowed to be resurrected, furthermore we had told all and sundry that any attempt to use it again would lead to an all out stoppage, what happened to the 500+ men from Wallis's? Yes you've got it again, dump them onto the N.D.L.B unattached pool. The shop stewards called a mass meeting to get the men to endorse the policy, I spoke to the men, probably speaking to passionately, but in all the years that I have represented the dockworkers this was the first time that I was asking for personal help on behalf of all the men who had been slung onto the unattached register.

Memories flashed back to me of a meeting between with Jimmy Reid and jimmy Airlie 2 of the men involved in the titanic work-in on the Upper Clyde ship builders, they told us over a glass of beer after a meeting, that redundancy brought the worst out of men, they went on to highlight instances, men who fought together in the war, men who would lay down their lives in helping out a comrade in trouble, blood relations who put their families above everything. Yet if you held a meeting of one hundred men and inform them that twenty of them were to be sacked, the outcome of the meeting would be no action as a majority of the 80 would actually believe that there job might be safer if they did not cause trouble. I dismissed this telling them that this was not the case in London, adding that the royal group of docks had a reputation that was second to none when it came to solidarity. They both raised their eyebrows expressing doubt, but without saying a word they left you in no doubt that they believed that you were wrong. I have to say that Jimmy Reid was one of the best orators I have had the privilege to hear.

The men at our meeting had given absolutely no indication of what was to follow; the meeting was seemingly going well when the chairman put the motion to be voted on. By an overwhelming majority they voted against the shop stewards recommendation, I could not believe it, they had voted selfishly, they had turned their backs on not just the shop stewards committee but over 500 men. I had to get away from the crowds that had formed to vent anger at what the men had just done, everyone was coming up with different solutions to try and get the men to change their minds. But at that moment I knew it was all over for me, I had never thought that this day would come, but it had and I was not feeling too clever. In fact I had to escape to a nearby toilet to be sick.

When the dust had settled and I had a chance to try and understand what the men had done, the picture was becoming worse, they had voted to try and protect their own jobs but instead they had unwittingly consigned themselves to the scrap heap. If we were feeling shocked by the men's decision then what do you think the employers and the government were thinking, it must have been out with the champagne and start making preparations to

Death of the Docks

finish of the job. So Jimmy Reid was right he had warned us that this type of vote will always be a possibility when redundancies are involved. How right he was. The trade unions also could not believe there luck, instead of another stoppage, that could have exposed everything that they had failed to do in solving the crisis in our Industry, they too had been granted an unexpected bonus in the shape of giving them more time to sort out the latest mess. The hundreds of men that Tom Wallis had carefully robbed and dumped felt not just let down but isolated, we had been to the trade unions to ask them to intervene and get the men an ex-gratia payment for all the men who had been robbed by Wallis, they assured us that they would take the matter up, more importantly we wanted to know what was going to happen to the men, we constantly reminded them that the unattached pool had yet again been resurrected in defiance of all the promises that had been made to our men. The Unions assured us that an emergency meeting of the London dock labour board was to take place, with only one item on the agenda, the immediate allocation of every man who was on the unattached pool. As for myself, I had decided that whilst the vote that took place after the official strike was a mortal blow, we had attempted to try and rebuild, however we never had time on our side, but this latest vote was unforgivable in my eyes. I had already decided at the ripe old age of 36 I was ready to turn it all in, I promised my long suffering Wife that never again would I get involved as I had done.

However, unlike many of my predecessors' I had no intentions of selling out, I would always remain on board the S. S Hardship. There would be no reward for me, no cushy little job with the union that I had attacked over the years. My place was and always will be alongside the working classes. But instead of being in the vanguard I would support and follow others. What happened next also changed the

Colin Ross

pattern of my life. Following the meeting of the London dock labour board every man had been re-allocated an Employer, this was done on a Pro-Rata basis, and existing Employers had to take men on the basis of how large there existing labour force was. Although at the time we were not informed but the allocations were purely temporary, and as people took up the severance offer the men would be sent to whatever company had the most men leaving.

I had been allocated along with 6 other men from Wallis's to a company operating the riverside agreement, the company was Purfleet deep wharf, the men who worked there enjoyed one of the highest rates of pay for dockworkers anywhere, however they had a very bad reputation, they had worked in several strikes and whilst there pay was high, they appeared to worship a pound note rather than join in actions that had taken place over the years. When the men who worked there heard that I had been allocated there, they had the audacity to hold a meeting and as a result informed the employer that they didn't mind the other 6 men who had been allocated but they did not want me to work there! This was what slag's they were. I never found out about this for a few weeks, but even before I went there, I went to both trade unions to make sure that the allocation had been done fairly and above board.

Sure enough on starting work at Purfleet I was made as welcome as a pork chop in a synagogue, because of my militant reputation they made it clear that I wasn't wanted. What they never realised was that I had absolutely no desire to be amongst them, the reputation that they had was a bad one, and although I had promised not to get involved any more they were not aware of this and saw me as a communist agitator. Nice to be wanted isn't it? Because of the attitude of the men, coupled with the message that the employer gave me informing me that I was to be the first

Death of the Docks

one that they wanted to get rid of,(the managing director of the place just happened to be chairman of the London Dock Labour Board) because of both of the attitudes of the employers and the men I decided to make it my business to stay there, again in hindsight this was a terrible move on my part. If my stubborn attitude hadn't kicked in I could have gone to work in Tilbury docks along with men who I could readily identify myself with.

The men who worked at Purfleet Deep Wharf in the main were the lowest form of human beings that I have ever encountered; their wages were 7 times more than what the enclosed docks were earning, when I picked up my first weeks wage packet I thought that I had won the lottery! I never knew such riches existed. Yet for all the money that they had at their disposal they had no time for the struggles of others, and two weeks into my penal sentence I heard that I was to be got rid of. Knowing that I would receive no support at all, I waited for the men to knock off for their tea break on the ship that was being unloaded and I went along the Jetty and removed all the fuses from the cranes. When they tried to resume work they discovered that I was sitting on the Jetty guarding the fuses, the top man was summoned and he appealed to me not to be silly, the union were called in by the employer. Because they had tried to just to get rid of me alone the company had to withdraw its request in letting me go. Because of my actions I received 4 days suspension, on my appeal hearing who do you think was sitting on the appeals panel?, The Chairman of the panel was my existing employer, and he was accompanied by Tom Wallis! And of course there was one union delegate. I could have employed Britain's top lawyer and still would have been transported to Botany Bay.

But they got the better of me (the men, not the employers) and in a bad moment I applied for the voluntary severance pay. What the little time that I had spent at Purfleet made me appreciate how decent men ,on a quarter of the money that these parasites were on, behaved with dignity and showed more courage than this lot could ever imagine. My application for the severance money seemed to have received top priority, the managing director of the toilet of a place where I worked called me up out of the ships hold to let me know that I was being released (A true description) on the following Friday. That fateful Friday, clutching my P45 and other bits and pieces I had 2or 3 glasses of beer with the 2 or 3 men who had stood by me at the place while I served my sentence at Purfleet Deep Wharf. The end was very sad for me; it was not like changing your job or retiring, this was the end of an era, the end of a way of life.

CONCLUSION

Many of you may well think that we got what we deserved, but I hope that just as many of you would have seen what we were up against and agree with me that the shipping companies, stevedoring contractors, local labour councils and governments from both sides of the political spectrum should hold their heads in shame. But these groups of people are usually the founder members of the "I'm Alright Jack brigade", so although you might expect people to do the decent thing, the truth is that these people would sell their Grandmother if the money was right.

Another lot who leave a great deal to be desired are "The Do Gooders", this minority group of middle class semi-professional people have an opinion on almost everything, usually the subject will have absolutely nothing to do with them, but they swamp the media and make their views known on the T.V &Radio. These people will tell you what's good for you; they will force their views on a whole spectrum of events on you, as long as the views don't interfere with their life style. But were where they when dockworkers were unloading huge amounts of asbestos? Where were they when dockworkers worked in conditions that would have been unacceptable 100 years ago? Yet alone today. Their silence was deafening.As for your local councillors well in the borough that covered the docks where I lived, the London Borough of Newham had 60 seats that made up the council and the labour party held 59 of these, so you could say that they could implement whatever they wanted without too much of a fight, were where they when it came to saving the dock industry? Well if you find out let me know, all they were interested in was getting their hands on huge chunks of land to develop. No different I hear you say to the motor industry, the mines, the shipbuilding industry, the merchant navy fleet, the steel Industry and a whole host of other Industries that made our country one of the leading industrial nations in the world, but what has the decimation of these once mighty Industries done to improve the lot of the workers who relied on them for a living? Not much I fear.

We had been victims' of modernisation, with none of the benefits going to our men, we had stemmed the tide with one of the best Industrial struggles that anyone could remember, it was brought to an end as a result of the anti-trade union laws, this took our campaign way of its original course, and when we tried to get it back on track we had shot our bolt. The establishment had won. The T.& G.W.U played a large role in undermining our campaign, much to their shame.

If I have not given the N.A.S&D.U(the blue union) the credit that they deserved then I apologise, for they always tried to help us, although they were initially against the introduction of the shop stewards, when the chips were down the Blue Union were there. Not being a member of the blue union stops me from knowing the workings like I know how the white union worked. What I do know is that the government and the kangaroo court in Chancery Lane never bothered them, they just carried on as if the court wasn't there yet in both cases involving Donaldson's court the Blue Union had a majority of members who were both threatened and imprisoned, still they never flinched. Maybe all dockworkers should have joined the blue union who only

Death of the Docks

represented us. You never saw them running around and panicking when Donaldson was on the rampage.

Despite the way it ended for me, I was proud to have been associated with the dock industry and the men who made the docks the place it was. I cannot comment on the finish as I had left the docks, and how it ended when the most evil prime minister this country has ever seen Margaret Thatcher removed the dockworkers registration, again the T&G.W.U let itself down.

In London we knew that not only did we face containerisation as a threat to our livelihoods, but a trip along where the once thriving docks where will tell you what the hierarchy had planned for the land that we obtained our living. The West India & Millwall docks have some wonderful riverside apartments with the new centre piece of Canary Wharf, strange isn't it? When Wapping was frequented by east enders the whole area was a rundown dustbin, no fancy wine bars or trendy restaurants' for us. Then we have what the royal docks have been turned into, first on the agenda we have the London City airport, huge exhibition centres ,massive housing projects, all the areas that the professional people have occupied have names that reflect the docks and the sea. So perhaps we won't be forgotten.

The heroic stand that Liverpool dockers made whilst the union totally sold them short, history will show that they had been given assurances by the then general secretary Bill Morris, he had delivered one of the finest speeches that you could ever wish to hear, **bringing** the house down, however making a fine speech is one thing but you must deliver the goods, Bill Morris and the T&G.W.U couldn't or wouldn't. As a result dear old Bill spent most of his remaining time as general secretary holed up like a scared rabbit in Transport House. Tragically before any of this took place Prime Minister Thatcher had set a trap for the miners, because of the grief that the miners had given the conservative governments, the evil woman from Downing Street had prepared plans to teach the miners and the whole trade union movement a lesson. It became apparent that if the working class stood by and allowed the miners to be beaten then the aftermath would include the dockers' registration.

Yet again the Trade Unions let not only there members down in doing next to nothing to assist the miners, but in the long run they had shot themselves in the foot, for the membership numbers of people belonging to trade unions would plummet. Ask anyone with an iota of common sense why we are Importing vast quantities of both oil and gas when we have years of coal just waiting to be taken from the ground. But common sense doesn't enter the equation when it comes to teaching a group of workers a lesson.I tried to do my bit to help the miners, but as I had become a self employed market trader selling fruit and vegetables I could hardly come out on strike, however I sent a huge quantity of fruit and veg to the Kent miners via some local teachers .This was only a small token, when after a struggle that lasted over a year, the miners were finally defeated it was only because of the most vicious and personal attack on an individual that this country has ever seen. Arthur Scargill was public enemy No. 1, it did not matter that what he was saying was 100% correct, he was right up there with the best of them, anyone seen with him was a communist plotter, an enemy of the state, and as for Arthur Scargill himself, because of the way the trade unions made him a social leper the cause of the miners was secondary to the "let's get Arthur brigade". The fact was and still is Arthur Scargill was right. Shame on every one of you, for all the hardship that you caused to good mining communities, may you rot with the devil.

As I draw to the end of my experiences in the Docks, I would like to pay the highest tribute to every dockworker

Death of the Docks

who I have had the privilege of both knowing them personally and having the honour to represent them against the dock employers. I say to every registered dockworker, hold your head high for you gave it everything, nobody else could have shown the fight that you did, you defied all the odds, and despite the continual onslaught from the media. Each and every one of you will have a wealth of memories, most of them good ones and even the not so good ones don't seem so bad when you dress them up a little and make light of them.

Registered dockworkers won't be found in Burke's peerages book nor will you find any of them listed in Who's Who, but had there been a working class equivalent then the roll of honour would have been crammed full of Dockers. I have paid my tributes to the finest group of men that I have ever known, as for the assortment of leaders that the dock threw up, I leave to you to judge them, and the one thing that I was proud of was the fact that the only group that I ever listened to was the men. Had more delegates followed this method of representing the men I am sure the outcome of events would have been totally different, for a start we would have picketed the L.I.F.T container base and I am sure given the momentum that had been built up, the only possible outcome would have been an outright victory. Throw that lot into the melting pot and the other container bases that would have followed suit and I am sure that today we would have had a registered dock labour force, given that we would have still had strength ,both industrially and numerically no government would have dared touch the registration. As it turned out it was not the employers who beat us nor was it the trade unions or the government, we shot ourselves in the foot by not being able to handle the situation after such a tremendous victory, had we all been able to remain focused on the struggle to regain our work then I know that this book would have a different ending.

Hindsight is always a wonderful thing, how many times have you said " if I only knew that this would turn out like it has I would have done it differently" , I can say with total honestly that I would have done exactly the same, given what I have discovered about some of the "ultra left wing" stewards and delegates they must have taken lessons from Brother John Prescott, some had more than one property, one even boasted a fine piano ,as for finance they made sure that they were in the big boys league when it come to looking after themselves. I don't subscribe to the they are wrong and I am right brigade, but I do that know that I was not wrong!   So I thank you if you have persevered and read my account of how we fought the system, I would have loved to have written in a happy ending but such is life.

I think Old Blue eyes can best sum me up, whatever mistakes I made I made them innocently, but as in all my life I did it my way.

FOOTNOTE

Since completing my account of how the Dock Industry was sold up the river by the Government, the Trade Unions and the ship owners it has come to light that our M.Ps have been caught with their fingers in the till. The situation is so serious that it almost turned into a constituenial crisis. The thefts that have come to light as a result of figures released under the freedom of information act range from a few thousand pounds up to several hundred thousands of pounds. It appears that most of the hierarchy of all the major parties have been de-frauding the British tax payer.

Ordinary people who normally would not listen or debate politics are livid with the very people who make the laws that govern our lives; this crisis has followed the crisis in the worlds banking system. The United Kingdom along with the good old U.S.A and a few more countries believed the cure for the banker's greed was to pump billions of pounds into the financial institutions, putting future generations into massive debt, a debt that will have to be repaid in the form of stringent income tax increases for as long as you can see, a debt that we have not accrued, in fact it is almost similar to identity theft, someone else has taken the money, spent it and done it in your name, the only benefit you get is that you have to repay it.

Our politicians have always been viewed with deep mistrust, but the expenses scandal shows the mentality of a bunch of spivs in suits, I must point out that a few M.Ps chose not to embark on the M.V Gravy train, to the credit of the few, there is still hope that the system may recover. However the leaders of the 3 main political parties do not appear to be blameless, it would appear that they have not led by example, or should I say that they plundered so much of the public purse it's a wonder that there is anything left.

Having been caught red handed the elected custodians of our country firstly offer to repay "some of the money that they had mistakenly taken", or had accepted under the rules of the House, the very same rules that they introduced! Now could you imagine what your employer would say to you if he caught you helping yourself to the companies funds, you inform him that you are prepared to put back some of the loot that somehow found its way into your bank account! Then if that don't work you then apologise, this is not for our M.Ps who regrouped and decided that the best form of defence is to attack! Their theme is "we have not done anything wrong". ......We know, don't we?

Lightning Source UK Ltd.
Milton Keynes UK
171087UK00001B/3/P